# WHAT TO DO WHEN SOMEONE HAS
## SOMEONE HAS
# DEBT PROBLEMS

*Uniform with this book*

# WHAT TO DO WHEN SOMEONE HAS DEBT PROBLEMS

## A PRACTICAL SURVIVAL GUIDE

by

JOHN MCQUEEN

PAPERFRONTS
**ELLIOT RIGHT WAY BOOKS**
**KINGSWOOD, SURREY, U.K.**

Made and Printed in Great Britain by Hunt Barnard Ltd, Aylesbury, Bucks.

# CONTENTS

# PART TWO

# DEDICATION

## TO MY WONDERFUL MOTHER AND FATHER

But for their love and courage,
I would not form part of this
universe.

If you lived in the richest, most powerful city it was possible
for a man to imagine, but there was no love there, no mercy
and no justice for those who met with misfortune; then you
would be better off dead than to live in such a place.

# INTRODUCTION

This book is intended to be a friend to people with debt problems. It outlines all the basic methods by which you should tackle dealing with your debt worries. You might also find it useful to help friends or relatives with their particular problems.

There is a long story behind the writing of this, my first book, and I hope the reader will take the trouble to read this introduction before hurrying on to read the practical advice I have been in a unique position to collect together.

During my own life I have experienced many occasions when debt burdens have dominated my thoughts. Debt burdens nearly always bring with them a sense of imprisonment. They also often bring a great sense of humiliation and frustration.

My own debt problems reached their peak when I attended University as a mature student at the age of 26. I had a wife and three young children to support and I soon found myself struggling to make ends meet out of my inadequate grant income. Somehow, I struggled through this difficult period, mainly by employing many of the strategies outlined in this book. So I write as someone who has directly experienced debt problems and not just as a comfortable observer.

The second part of this book deals with bankruptcy, something I have thankfully not experienced at first-hand. However I watched my brother James go through the full trauma of personal bankruptcy, and became so concerned and upset by what he experienced, that I founded the Association of Bankrupts early in 1983 to help debtors and bankrupts.

Since then I have been contacted by literally thousands of people who have either gone bankrupt or who are in serious debt. Some of their experiences are briefly outlined in the final chapter of this book. I have met many of them personally. Indeed many of them are now my friends. So I know a great deal about the practical side of debt problems and going bankrupt, and of the psychological consequences.

This book is therefore firmly based on what actually happens in all the situations described within it and I have been careful to check the detail. There is one area where the text is a little less comprehensive. This is the short chapter on Scotland. I believe this book will be nearly as useful to Scottish readers as to English and Welsh ones but I apologise to Scotland that lack of space prevents a fuller explanation of how practice may differ there.

My involvement with debt problems has led me to think carefully about the way we treat debtors in Great Britain. While it is true that the debtors' prisons of the Victorian period are long since a thing of the past, attitudes towards debtors remain peculiarly harsh, especially towards bankrupts. We tend to label anyone in serious debt in Great Britain as some sort of criminal, and this increases the feelings of degradation that most debtors feel.

In the United States such attitudes are unheard of. In contrast, over there some venture capitalists are even unlikely to back an entrepreneur unless he has been involved in at least one or two failures, on the basis that only then will he have learned how to avoid such mistakes.

The general debt burden on the average household in Britain has doubled in the last decade and is likely to increase further as our consumer society pushes easy credit at us to buy goods. Our economy now revolves, it seems, on people obtaining credit to buy goods. One unfortunate consequence of easy credit has been to reduce the value of second-hand goods. Who wants to buy anything second-hand when for a small deposit you can have the brand new article? This fact erodes the value of our household assets such as furniture and electrical equipment. Many items lose much of their worth from the moment they are purchased.

At the time of writing new insolvency legislation is being debated by Parliament. This new legislation recognises the Victorian nature of our existing legislation, but very few significant changes are likely to emerge.

The need to protect society against irresponsible and or crooked bankrupts seems to be foremost in legislators' minds, despite the fact that such people invariably find ways round whatever laws are made anyway. I fear that as a result, and also because vested interests of big business hog the limelight whenever changes are mooted, our system of dealing with debtors will still remain inadequate for the ordinary individuals who get into serious debt. I sincerely hope that some future government will tackle this area of law properly and provide these decent people with a "safe harbour" where their difficulties can be resolved fairly and in an atmosphere of genuine and humane social concern.

I would like to thank the Elliot brothers for "discovering me", and for having the foresight to publish this book. I would particularly thank Malcolm Elliot for his encouraging interest and faith in me.

I also have in mind as I write, my grandfather William O'Mara, who went bankrupt in the twenties, but who successfully rebuilt his steeplejack business before he died. My other grandfather, James McQueen, left his family after the First World War to roam around Scotland. He entered Scottish folklore as the "Rovin Boy". It was said that he rarely had a penny to his name but was always contented.

My parents are mentioned in the dedication, but I am also thinking there of my wife Jean, and my ten brothers and sisters. I am blessed with so much love. Special thoughts are due too, for those deep down people and friends who have filled my life. I would be failing in my duty if I made no mention of my three teenage sons, John, Andrew, and Stephen, who make sure that I am always kept on my toes.

Lastly, thanks to Judy and Bronwen for doing the typing.

J. M.
Lancaster.

# PART ONE

# 1

## BEING REALISTIC

It is very easy to get into serious debt; much more difficult is to pull yourself out of it. If you are in debt you must become ruthlessly realistic about your money.

The first task is to turn yourself into an accountant and draw up a balance sheet. You need two sheets of paper. On one make a list of your weekly or monthly income and expenditure; on the other, list all your assets and your debts. e.g. MR & MRS ECCLES – 3 CHILDREN AGED 7, 9 and 13

| INCOME (WEEKLY AFTER TAX) | | EXPENDITURE (WEEKLY) | |
|---|---|---|---|
| Wages (Mr Eccles) | £224.00 | Food | £43.00 |
| Child benefit | £25.00 | Mortgage | £40.50 |
| | | Rates | £8.00 |
| | | Electricity | £15.00 |
| | | Gas | £4.00 |
| | | Telephone | £6.00 |
| | | TV & video hire | £5.50 |
| | | Clothes | £15.00 |
| | | Milk | £6.00 |
| | | Papers | £2.00 |

|  |  |
|---|---|
| House insurance (building contents, and mortgage protection policies) | £3.00 |
| Car running costs | £18.00 |
| Cigarettes | £10.00 |
| Entertainment | £27.00 |
| Miscellaneous household | £17.00 |
| Mr Eccles' life assurance | £16.00 |
| Debts' repayments | £78.00 |

| | | | |
|---|---|---|---|
| Total | £249.00 | Total | £314.00 |

Thus on the income and expenditure side, Mr and Mrs Eccles are spending £65 per week more than is coming into the household. This has been going on for some time creating a debt position which, if they do not deal with it, has the potential to overwhelm them. Having looked at their income and expenditure, they now need to look at their assets and debts.

| ASSETS | | DEBTS | |
|---|---|---|---|
| House (now reckoned conservatively at) | £30,000 | Mortgage (left to pay from £21,000 originally) | £16,000 |
| Furniture | £3,000 | HP – calculated from | |
| Car | £2,400 | number of equal | |
| Building society | £250 | instalments still due: | |
| Coin collection | £250 | Furniture | £1,100 |
| Antiques | £650 | Car (original price £3,500) | £2,500 |

| | | | |
|---|---|---|---|
| Insurance policy (surrender value) | £800 | Credit card debt (his plus hers) | £2,300 |
| | | Personal loan for redecoration and fitted carpets (balance left to pay off) | |
| | £37,350 | | £2,500 |

But – to allow for what you always lose when you have to sell things – say:

| | | | |
|---|---|---|---|
| Total | £33,500 | Total | £24,400 |

Mr & Mrs Eccles are fortunate enough to be buying their own home which through inflation has risen in value since they moved in. If they were to sell their house they could clear their debts. However this would leave them with the problem of finding somewhere else to live. The children are all settled in a nearby school so the Eccles family would find moving very upsetting. They also have a pleasant home in an area they enjoy living in.

Mr & Mrs Eccles need to ask themselves two basic questions:
1) Can we increase our income?
2) Can we spend less?

## Can We Increase Our Income?

Mr Eccles might try asking his boss for a rise or seek a position with higher earnings. Mrs Eccles could consider a part-time job. Mr Eccles should check with his employer or tax office that his tax code is correct and he is getting his full allowances, and Mrs Eccles with the Social Security (DHSS) office that she is getting her full entitlement to state benefits. A leaflet, revised regularly by the government, sets out all the benefits currently in payment. It is called "Which Benefit?" and can be obtained from your local social security office. Get an up-to-date one to see that you are claiming all those benefits which apply to you.

If Mrs Eccles was able to get a part-time job straightaway this couple could probably easily bring their debt problems under control without any drop in their standard of living. That is not always so easy, so let us move on.

## Can We Spend Less?

The great advantage of drawing up a balance sheet is that you make yourselves look where your money is going. Many people simply have no idea how much they spend on what. Then you can investigate each item individually and see what you can do to reduce it.

Nevertheless these are very personal decisions. Mr & Mrs Eccles have always managed a reasonable standard of living. For several years, however, they have not been able to take a family holiday, and with the increasing expense of bringing up three growing children they have gradually run into debt. We continue their appraisal with them.

**Food:** It is so important people feed themselves properly that this item should suffer the least cut-backs. However, Mrs Eccles decides that as the family is being fed a good, wholesome, basic diet she can reduce the family food bill by a modest £2 through cutting out unnecessary cakes, biscuits and sweets which have little nourishment value anyway.

**Mortgage:** If Mr Eccles has a good record with his building society the best solution to his problems may lie here. Provided he goes to see them early and puts all his cards on the table, they may look favourably at increasing the size of his mortgage and perhaps extending the number of years it will run. If they approve his overall plans for resolving his major borrowings (we see shortly how he intends to raise cash by other means to pay off some of these loans), they might agree to increase his mortgage sufficiently for him to reach a position where he can pay off all his other debts. They may even help enough to make some of his more drastic possible actions unnecessary. He is thus enabled to swap his high interest rate debts for an increased mortgage at its advantageously low rate of interest. With the repayments stretching out so much further too, his weekly debt burden drops dramatically. In such a case the building society may well feel happier to have someone now in a position to repay his slightly higher mortgage reliably, than a person saddled with so much high priced debt that even his existing repayments are in jeopardy.

Obviously you are not likely to receive such help more than once and the possibilities may be limited by your salary, the present value of your home etc. For the sake of this example and to make it more comparable with someone who is not buying his own home we will assume that Mr Eccles has already been refused further assistance from this source.

**Electricity:** A look at Chapter 5 will almost certainly give several ideas about how to reduce this item. The Eccles find that some lagging, installing a special meter to obtain cheap-rate overnight electricity and some extra care make a net weekly saving of £1.50.

**Gas:** As they have a new fuel-efficient gas fire they decide the only thing they can hope to do is to save 50p a week by being especially careful.

**TV & Video:** The Eccles rent a TV and video. They decide they can do without the video and actually buy a new TV at a cost of £3.00 per week against the £5.50 going out at the moment.

**Clothes:** They agree that there is little they can do about cutting the cost of clothing although Mrs Eccles reckons that if she checks for competitive prices a bit more she can save £1 per week.

**Milk:** With three young children, Mr & Mrs Eccles decide they are not prepared to reduce their expenditure on milk.

**Papers:** Mr & Mrs Eccles decide to cancel their daily papers, which included a delivery charge. As they do not often read them anyway they will buy the occasional paper when they feel like it instead. They estimate this should save £1 per week.

**Life assurance:** Mr Eccles discovers that only a small portion of his life assurance premium provides him with the necessary life cover; the rest is actually a savings plan. He checks with an insurance broker and finds that for straightforward life cover only, he can obtain more than twice as much protection for his family for a small fraction of the weekly premium being paid on the savings plan. He decides this alternative will have to suffice, both because he needs the surrender value to raise cash (£800) and because it will reduce his weekly outlay by £12. The surrender value is substantially less than he paid in because of the penalties for early surrender but he has little choice.

**Car running costs:** Mr Eccles needs a car to travel to work. They regard the car as an essential family getabout but decide they will swap the luxury of their regular Sunday afternoon spin for some less expensive activity in future. Keeping to essential use only of the car will save at least £3 per week.

**Cigarettes:** Mr Eccles smokes too much and he knows it. Mrs Eccles, who smokes an occasional cigarette, promises to give up altogether if Mr Eccles vows to cut down. Apart from improving their health they agree they can save £5.50 per week to start with and more later if Mr Eccles can eventually give up.

**Entertainment:** Most of this is spent on drinks, either at home or when Mr Eccles goes to the pub. They decide they can save £5 per week here and that this cut can only improve their health too.

**Miscellaneous:** Mrs Eccles estimates that by being rigorously selective in dealing with the irregular items of expenditure that crop up in every household she can save £1 a week.

Altogether they work out that by tightening their expenditure they can save £35 per week. This still leaves them continuing to run into further debt at the rate of £30 per week.

The next thing that Mr & Mrs Eccles need to do is to see if they can dispose of any assets to reduce their debts and thus the weekly repayments' burden.

**House:** They know they can sell the house and repay everything but they would then have to buy another or rent one, with all the consequent upheaval. Had the house been much too big or in far too expensive an area, they might have looked around to see possibilities. As it is neither of those they decide that keeping hold of it is a priority and that they would only sell it as a last, desperate act.

**Furniture:** Mr & Mrs Eccles make a survey of their furniture. Not much seems to be unnecessary. Even if they sold some it would not really fetch much. They conclude that there is not really anything that they can achieve by disposing of furniture.

**Car:** They discuss the need to have the present car. Mr Eccles accepts that they could manage with a cheaper one. He knows his present car should fetch at least £2,400 and agrees to replace it with one costing £1,500 until their situation improves. Early settlement of the present HP contract will cost £2,000. This is a good figure. As there will be a new contract with the same finance company they have waived the normal early settlement penalty (see page 43). So they will have £400 in hand. However, on a car costing £1,500 there will be at least £600 deposit to pay and the length of the contract will have to be shorter. This is because the car is older. Nevertheless on the new loan which will be for £900 the repayments should only come to around half as much per week.

**Building society:** They decide that the £250 they have in the building society must remain there in case of emergency.

**Coin collection:** Mr Eccles had a coin collection left to him by his grandfather which is of great sentimental value to him. His wife agrees this should only be sold in dire emergency.

**Antiques:** Mr & Mrs Eccles have a small number of antiques collected when they first got married in which they have since lost interest. They decide to sell them and apply the money towards paying off the HP on the furniture.

**Life assurance:** As explained Mr Eccles has already decided to cash this in.

Altogether by these measures, Mr & Mrs Eccles find that, leaving aside the mortgage, they can cut their total capital debts by approximately one third. The £1,850 raised in cash pays off the furniture HP (£950 early settlement), and in addition enables them to put down the deposit of £600 on the cheaper car as well as to pay off £300 of their credit card debts. After allowing for their new HP contract on the replacement car these moves reduce their burden of weekly debt repayments by as much as £34.

The Eccles implement their decisions and soon begin to have a few pounds over each week, instead of rising debts. Sensibly, they apply their spare cash to the next priority, that of reducing their credit card debts further.

By taking such realistic action, Mr & Mrs Eccles should ultimately overcome their debt problems, though a few pounds in hand per week to speed the process is precious little margin if unexpected expenses give them a knock. The cheaper car will finish being paid for sooner and release more money to speed up repayments of the other debts. However, there is obviously an increased risk of expensive repairs having to be made to an older car.

If they had failed to take such action they could quite soon have found themselves in a position from which it would have been difficult, if not impossible, to extricate themselves. Mr & Mrs Eccles were fortunate in being able to reduce their debts both through having assets that they could dispose of and the alternative of running a less expensive car. They also had the surplus value of their home to back them up if things came to the crunch. Other people are not so fortunate as the Eccles. You may be one of them. Consider the following example:

## MR & MRS LIVINGSTONE – TWO CHILDREN AGED 2 and 4

| INCOME (WEEKLY AFTER TAX) | | EXPENDITURE (WEEKLY) | |
|---|---|---|---|
| Wages | | | |
| (Mr Livingstone) | £75.00 | Food | £30.00 |
| Child benefit | £18.00 | Rent/Rates | £15.00 |
| | | Electricity | £6.00 |
| | | Gas | £5.00 |
| | | Clothes | £6.00 |
| | | Milk | £5.00 |
| | | Home insurance | £1.00 |
| | | Cigarettes | £3.00 |
| | | Entertainment | £7.00 |
| | | Miscellaneous | £6.00 |
| | | Debt repayments | £30.00 |
| Total | £93.00 | Total | £114.00 |

Mr & Mrs Livingstone need an extra £21 income to meet their needs. They have neglected to claim all the benefits (other than child benefit) to which a family on such low income are entitled. They must sort this out at once in the same way the Eccles family were advised on page 17. Always short of income, their assets and debts are in a much worse state than those of the Eccles family.

| ASSETS | | DEBTS (still outstanding) | |
|---|---|---|---|
| House (rented) | Nil | HP (furniture) | £800 |
| Furniture | £2,200 | Money lender | £3,500 |
| Total (under the hammer) say: | £800 | Total | £4,300 |

In this case there are no assets that they could manage without. Nor, on such a tight budget, can the Livingstones save much on their household expenditure. They might cut back on entertainment and cigarettes, but this would not make ends meet and would reduce them to leading the life of paupers.

Mr Livingstone has fallen into the hands of a money lender from time to time, forced to borrow money to meet the shortfall in income. Although he has probably long since repaid most of the capital, with its very high interest rate the debt just keeps on growing with little or no chance of Mr Livingstone ever catching up. Mr & Mrs Livingstone are extremely worried. Mrs Livingstone is on drugs from her doctor to calm her nerves caused by the worry. They are at their wits' end. The money lender has a fellow who calls weekly, pestering them beyond reason for payments that they have fallen behind with.

The next thing the Livingstones must do is to deal with the intimidation they are experiencing from the money lender's representative as outlined in Chapter 3. They could also write to the money lender telling the firm that they intend to stop making any further payments, and suggesting they take Court action about the matter if they so wish. This will enable the Livingstones to ask for a realistic repayment schedule to be ordered under the protection of the Court. Having a judgment order should bring an end to much of the pressure. People in serious debt should not always view Courts as "the enemy"; very often they can be friend and protector. Another example might be granting an administration order to the Livingstones. See Chapter 10.

If the agent from the money lender has been threatening to make the Livingstones bankrupt they should not worry. It would cost the money lender plenty, with little hope of any return. He could not normally do it until after they had failed to pay a judgment order in any case. If he was able to, then in the Livingstones' case even this might be a partial blessing. If you are in the Livingstones' situation start the actions advised in this book immediately. Doing so will itself help you to stop worrying. Tackled properly, most domestic debt problems can be resolved.

In our last example now, we look at a family where the extent of the problems probably means bankruptcy has become inevitable. People in this unenviable position often fail to recognise what is coming and put themselves through appalling misery in desperate hope of resolving the impossible. It is no use ignoring reality. If your financial predicament cannot be restored, the sooner you admit it to yourself the better.

## MR & MRS UNFORTUNATE (NO CHILDREN)

| INCOME (MONTHLY AFTER TAX) | | EXPENDITURE (MONTHLY) | |
|---|---|---|---|
| Mr Unfortunate | £700.00 | Rent | £300.00 |
| Mrs Unfortunate | £350.00 | Other expenses | £700.00 |
| | | Debt repayments | £580.00 |
| Total | £1,050.00 | Total | £1,580.00 |

| ASSETS | | DEBTS | |
|---|---|---|---|
| House (rented) | Nil | Mr Unfortunate | £21,000 |
| Furniture | £1,500 | Mrs Unfortunate | £4,000 |
| Car (owned by Mr Unfortunate's employer) | Nil | In joint names | £2,500 |
| Total (under the hammer) say: | £500 | Total | £27,500 |

This scale of debt quite often arises out of divorce. Mr & Mrs Unfortunate were both previously married. When they married each other, each brought with them heavy debts which have built up into an impossible burden.

Unless a legacy or the pools save him Mr Unfortunate is

bound to go bankrupt because his debts are so large. Of the monthly expenses £200 a month is maintenance for his children of his first marriage. His debts are huge because they include the mortgage he is keeping up so that his former wife and their offspring can stay in the home they are used to.

Bankruptcy for Mrs Unfortunate may yet be avoidable. If they can find cheaper accommodation, cut other expenses to the bone, and keep his creditors at bay for long enough, scrimping and saving every other available penny towards getting the joint debts and her own debts down below figures worth being sued for, she may escape the indignities of bankruptcy. This is worth fighting for by every legal means in this book. See Part Two.

Very often people in Mr & Mrs Unfortunate's position fail to see that their situation is out of control. Refusal to accept the inevitable, or daily escalating worry seem to cloud judgment and they struggle on for too long, only to meet bankruptcy anyway. If you think that your financial position may be beyond redemption, or you are uncertain, act now. Do not keep all your anxiety bottled up inside you. Discuss all the facts with your family or a reliable friend. See if your conclusions are unavoidable, or if they can support you in a sound, workable plan.

The simple action of sharing the worry, itself helps you to re-focus on reality and what to do. Win or lose, treat yourself to the much needed prop it represents.

In some large cities you may find a money advice centre you can go to. Check with a library or Citizens Advice Bureau. The CAB itself may have an experienced debt counsellor.

You might prefer to have some confidential advice through contacting the Association of Bankrupts, founded by the author of this book. The address is: ASSOCIATION OF BANKRUPTS, 4 Johnson Close, Abraham Heights, Lancaster, LA1 5EU. The Association exists to provide specialist help to people who are in extremely difficult financial circumstances and who do not know which way to turn. It also maintains a list of accountants and solicitors around the country who are prepared to advise debtors for a very small charge, or no charge at all.

After reading this Chapter you may be tempted to head quickly for a specific subject. The Contents or Index should lead swiftly to what you want. However, when a battle for solvency is in progress, I recommend fighting on all fronts available. Even if you assume there is nothing to be done on some of the debts involved, there may be good moves to make. So do look at every Chapter at all relevant to your interests, and, especially, do read the general Chapters on negotiating with creditors (7), claiming benefits (8), what happens in the Courts (10) – they can be a help to debtors in some circumstances – and, who can go bankrupt (12).

# 2

# RENT, MORTGAGE AND RATE ARREARS

**Rent Arrears**

The easiest thing in the world when money is short is to miss paying the rent one week. As a result many millions of people are constantly behind in their rent payments. This applies to private tenants and council tenants alike. These arrears can soon build up to a point where they seem impossible to repay and become a major source of worry.

Eventually your landlords, whether they are private or council, will sue you to get possession for their property. They can go to the Court and ask for an eviction order. If you are behind with your rent payments a Court has virtually no option but to grant an eviction order which means you must leave the property by a date set by the Court. If you do not leave the property by the date set then Court officials can forcibly evict you.

If you are evicted from your home, you may then find it extremely difficult to rent another property. Councils are not necessarily obliged to rehouse you if you have been evicted for rent arrears, and most private landlords would ask for a reference from your previous landlord.

Therefore being evicted is something to be avoided at all costs.

While the basic problems facing council tenants and private tenants with rent arrears are the same, there are differences between the two types of tenancy which need to be dealt with separately.

## Council Tenants

A council tenant is someone who lives in public property, owned and controlled by the local council. The local council is democratically elected and is usually very responsible and caring in its attitude towards tenants with rent arrears. Many councils employ rent collectors who call round weekly or fortnightly to collect the rent. If you fall into arrears the first thing to do is to explain the reasons why to the rent collector. The rent collector can then report back to his manager so that the council are made aware of your problems.

Arrangements might be made so that you can pay off the rent arrears by making small extra payments in addition to your normal rent. This way your arrears are gradually reduced. If your arrears are very great and seem impossible to repay, then a few councils are prepared to write-off part of the debt, so long as some effort is made to pay off the arrears. The important point is at least to pay the usual rent at this stage. Very few councils would move to evict a tenant who was not allowing rent arrears to build up any further.

It might be that, because of your circumstances, you still find it difficult to pay even the usual rent. In this case it would be worthwhile to give some careful thought to the house you are living in. You may be occupying a home that is too large for your needs and paying a larger rent than you need to. Many old people often live alone in large council houses when they would be better off, and happier, in a small flat. Give careful thought to your housing needs and ask the council for advice. If you ask your rent collector or telephone the housing department at your local council someone will come round to discuss your needs and problems.

A council tenant can also go directly to a local councillor, who has been elected to represent the local people. If you do not know the name of your local councillor, then ask one of your neighbours. If they do not know, then telephone the local council. The person on the switchboard will put you through to someone who can help you. Do not be uneasy about going to see your local councillor. Most councillors are public spirited people who are only too pleased to help.

They can talk to public officials at the council on your behalf and they may well find a solution to your problems. They can sometimes pull strings for you by persuading council officials of the urgency of your problems. Discuss with your councillor the problems you are having paying the rent. It may be that your home is particularly expensive to heat. Perhaps there are other council properties available which are much cheaper to heat and maintain as well as having a lower rent.

Perhaps you are in difficulties with your rent because you are in a low paid job. In this case you might well be entitled to help towards paying your rent and you should carefully read through Chapter 8, which explains how to go about claiming your proper benefits. This alone may solve your main financial difficulties.

In certain parts of the country you may find cheaper privately rented housing but this is extremely rare. Council subsidised housing is usually the cheapest alternative. It would also be difficult to find a private landlord who would rent a house to someone already in arrears of their rent with a local council. So every effort should be made to reach a solution with the council concerned.

If you find you are not getting the assistance you hoped for from the people already mentioned, then write a clear, concise letter to your Member of Parliament. He or she may be prepared to intervene on your behalf. Members of Parliament are privileged and important people whose views are taken very seriously. Again, ask a neighbour for the name of your Member of Parliament if you do not know it. You can then write directly to him or her, c/o the House of Commons, London, SW1A 0AA. Get someone to help you with the letter if you have difficulty in writing. Or, you may prefer to go and meet your Member of Parliament at a surgery, which most of them hold regularly in their local constituencies. They are called surgeries because they provide a time and a place for people to discuss their problems with their Members of Parliament in the same way they discuss problems with their doctor. These are usually advertised in the local paper with a number to ring to make an appointment. Or, the MP's local constituency office can tell you if and when they are held. Do not be afraid to contact your Member of Parliament. They are elected and paid to serve all their constituents regardless of party – so that includes you.

## Private Tenants

A private tenant is a person who rents housing from someone other than a public authority. Private landlords are usually much stricter about rent arrears, often because they depend on the rental income for their own living. Private landlords therefore tend to be much less sympathetic towards tenants who get into arrears. Understandably, few of them will allow large rent arrears to build up and some will move quickly for an eviction order.

If a landlord calls personally to collect the rent the situation is one of straightforward face-to-face negotiation. Some landlords will be sympathetic to people faced with short-term problems, and, like some councils, they might be prepared to write-off some rent arrears.

Do not try and hide from your landlord, for example by arranging to be "out" when he usually calls. This will only increase his anger and the likelihood of an eviction order being sought more swiftly.

Some private tenants never meet their landlords, and scarcely know who they are. Those landlords who own many properties often employ agents to manage their properties for them and to collect rents. Estate agents may be used for this purpose. The same rule applies about keeping these agents informed of your situation. Treat them as though they are your landlord because they often make the decision, on his behalf, about whether to go for an eviction order or not.

Rents in the private sector vary a great deal but are generally higher than rents paid for council property. There are laws that control the amount of rent that you should pay. If you feel you are paying too much rent, then you should contact your local council and ask to speak to the officer who is responsible for fair rents in your district. This official will inspect your rented property and can have the rent reduced if he feels it is too much.

Some landlords try to get round these regulations by letting out property supposedly as "holiday accommodation" or as "short-term lets". This enables them to avoid fair rent laws. You should try to get out of the hands of such landlords as soon as possible. See your local councillor or Citizens Advice Bureau to find out if they can help. Your landlord might be acting unlawfully. It is worth checking out.

A private tenant can also search round to try and find cheaper accommodation. People renting accommodation of very similar types can often be paying very different rents. Some church organisations and other charitable bodies rent houses and flats at very moderate rents, whilst other private landlords may be seeking to obtain the highest rents that the market will stand. It is well worth carefully looking into what other rented accommodation might be available. Ask friends and neighbours if they know of any possibilities. Also visit some estate agents and let them know the sort of place you are looking for and the range of rent you are prepared to pay.

Every private tenant would also be well advised to contact the housing department of their local council. There might not be a suitable property available immediately but all councils maintain lists of people hoping to be housed by the council. Usually a points system is used whereby points are given depending on your needs – such as how many children you might have. Points may also be given for the length of time you have been on the list. Those people with the highest points get their needs attended to first so it is important to get your name registered on any list that might exist. Once you are on this list you should write a letter every few months to the housing manager reminding him of your need. If your circumstances change, such as with a new baby being born, then let him know immediately. Again, if you are really desperate, you should try to enlist the support of a local councillor.

Do everything you possibly can to tackle the situation. If you fall into rent arrears and just sit back hoping the problem will go away, it will simply get worse. Take no action and you will hasten the evil day when an eviction order is served, bringing with it a whole lot more problems which might have been avoided.


## Notice To Quit

If you do reach the unhappy stage of receiving a notice to quit because you are in arrears with your rent do not ignore it. If you do you will quickly find yourself on the street. Whether you are a private tenant or a council tenant contact your landlord immediately. It might still be possible to reach an agreement to deal with the arrears and to avoid the need for Court action. If you cannot reach an agreement with your landlord you will receive a Court summons telling you to attend Court. With it will come a form of admission, or defence, which you should complete and return.

If you dispute the amount of money your landlord says you owe or if you have a counterclaim, e.g. for repairs, then you will need to seek some advice on how to counterclaim. You should contact a solicitor and check if you can obtain free legal aid. Your solicitor will tell you if you are likely to qualify for legal aid and will give you the necessary forms. A Citizens Advice Bureau may be able to help you. Some have full-time employees who may be prepared to do all the paperwork for you, or even speak for you in the Court. Others depend on the help of voluntary part-time workers. The latter will still be able to advise you about legal aid, and will possibly be able to recommend a solicitor. Citizens Advice Bureaux make no charge for the service they provide.

Whatever happens make sure you attend the Court hearing and arrive there in good time. Court hearings are sometimes very formal affairs but there is no need to be frightened of attending. You can be sure that the registrar (judge) who hears the case will be very fair. However, if you do not attend the hearing without explanation, the registrar may take it for granted that you are not interested in the outcome of the case.

If you attend the Court hearing it is very likely that the registrar or judge will make a suspended order. This means you will be able to stay in your home as long as you pay the weekly or monthly rent, plus an amount off the arrears, which the Court will fix after hearing about your circumstances.

Make sure you or the solicitor, or the person speaking on your behalf, tell the registrar all about your financial circumstances and the maximum amount that you can afford to pay. Registrars and judges do not enjoy evicting people from their home and are likely to accept any reasonable offer that you might make.

If after the Court hearing you find you still cannot afford to make the payment agreed to, go back to your landlord and see if you can make a lower repayment. Your landlord will probably agree in order to avoid all the trouble of another Court hearing. Even if you are taken to Court again you will still be able to ask the registrar to agree to a lower repayment being made. The essential thing if you are still in difficulty is not to allow arrears to build up any further, otherwise the registrar will be forced to grant an eviction order and you will find yourself out on the street.

**Mortgage Arrears**

Many millions of people are buying their own homes by means of a mortgage from a building society, or a bank. A few people have private mortgages, whereby a relative or a friend provides the money.

People fall into arrears with their mortgages for all sorts of reasons. You may have been made redundant or your family circumstances might have changed. The interest rate being charged for your mortgage could have increased recently to the point that you cannot afford the new repayment level.

Whatever the reason for falling into arrears the problem remains the same and has got to be tackled in a sensible way. As in the case of rent arrears it is important that you let your building society or bank know of your problems immediately. (Sometimes a building society will suspend or reduce repayments for a time, for example if a man is laid off during a strike, so don't be afraid to ask.) If you simply stop making payments and ignore reminders you will find that within a few months you will be summoned to the Court for a possession order.

If a Court grants a possession order on your property this means you will have to leave the property by a date set by the Court unless you appeal immediately against the decision. The property will then be sold to pay off the mortgage. The costs of making the sale will be deducted before the balance is applied to paying off the mortgage. If the sale of the property does not raise enough to pay off the whole of the mortgage you will have to pay off the balance. Compared with a normal sale, you stand to lose a substantial chunk of capital in a forced sale of this kind. This is because the building society will be keen to recoup as much of the money it lent you as quickly as possible in order to lend it out again. Your house may well be sold to the first person who makes an offer for your property, which is likely to be for a smaller sum than you could hold out for if you sold your house under normal conditions.

Therefore at all costs, action should be taken to avoid a possession order and its unpleasant consequences. Every building society and bank will have its own policies of dealing with problems of this sort and some of them may be less sympathetic than others. An agreement that might hold with one building society or bank may not suffice with another. The circumstances surrounding each individual case are likely to vary greatly. There will be differences in the ages of people, the amounts outstanding, and the length of mortgage periods left to run. The solution to your particular problem will therefore have to be tailor-made to meet your personal needs.

Before looking at some individual examples there are some basic guidelines that are bound to help in all cases. If you are in arrears but are now in the position whereby you can continue to make the normal repayments regularly, do so. If you can afford to pay off part of the arrears as well, however small, then so much the better. It is hard to imagine that any building society or bank would take further action against someone who was clearly making an effort either to hold the arrears in check, or, better still, who was gradually reducing them.

Go along and see your building society manager or bank manager to discuss the situation. You might prefer to telephone if you find it difficult to make a personal visit. In such a discussion stick to the facts that affect your financial circumstances. Recounting a long list of all your personal troubles is likely to reduce sympathy for you, not increase it. Explain clearly for example, that you have lost your job, or that specific recent heavy bills for fuel have left you short on your mortgage repayments. A simple explanation is always the best.

After any meeting or telephone discussion write a letter setting out what you have agreed to. This saves any confusion or disagreement that might arise later. People often have different memories of the same conversation. So put what you agreed to in writing, and keep a copy. You will be respected for it.

The kind of agreements that can be made over mortgage arrears, can include substantial re-arrangements in appropriate circumstances. Take the case of a young family where the husband was made redundant and is many months behind with his mortgage payments but he has recently obtained a new job. His pay is lower than that of his previous job and he finds that not only is he unable to make any payments off the arrears but he is also unable to pay the normal repayment. He had a twenty year mortgage which had been paid regularly for six years before he was made redundant. Because the man is young it may well be possible to re-arrange completely the original agreement to repay the mortgage. In effect, the existing debt that has built up is put together, and becomes the subject of a new mortgage. The debt can then be repaid over a new period of twenty or even twenty-five years. The period over which repayments are made is thus extended and the monthly repayments will be smaller. There is no guarantee that an agreement of this sort can be reached but it is well worth trying if this means you can avoid losing your home.

If you have an endowment type mortgage rather than an

ordinary repayment mortgage you might experience greater difficulties rearranging repayments because endowment mortgages are tied into insurance contracts. This is one reason amongst many to avoid endowment-linked mortgages. If you are locked into one you will need to discuss with the building society or bank the possibilities of changing the type of mortgage you have. This is just another unfortunate hurdle you will have to overcome but it can be done so check out all the possibilities.

Always make contact with your building society or bank manager to talk about your problems at the time they arise. As discussed in Chapter 1, a larger, or longer term, mortgage may solve a lot of your problems. Too often people fail to talk with the people who can help or leave it all too late. If your building society is not told by you – you can be sure that no-one else will tell them.

It is pointless to ignore warning letters regarding mortgage arrears. The problem will not go away. The longer you ignore reminder letters the sooner the day will arrive when you are presented with a Court possession order. Believe me, any solution to your problem is better than being dispossessed of your home under a Court order. It may be that you could manage to repay a smaller mortgage on a cheaper house if you sold your present home. Perhaps you will decide to rent somewhere until your finances are back on a sounder footing.

So long as the building society or bank are informed that your property is for sale and kept in touch with progress, they are most unlikely to press you for arrears or to try to obtain a possession order. There is no need for them to do so because you are solving the problem for them. If you discuss the situation fully with the manager, he might well be happy to provide you with a smaller mortgage that you can afford to repay on another property. The longer you put off discussing mortgage arrears the more difficult it will be for you. Confidence in yourself will be lost and you will find it much more difficult to obtain the help you need.

The last thing in the world you want is for your home to become the subject of a possession order. This will make it extremely difficult to obtain a mortgage again in the future. Also your credit rating is likely to suffer elsewhere because so many credit agencies keep lists of Court orders that have been made against people. So whatever happens do not just sit back and let things hit you. If your position is so difficult that you cannot solve your problems by one of the methods suggested and you are bound to lose your home, at least take some positive action. Contact the housing department at your local council and explain your situation to them fully. You can then sort out in advance the necessary arrangements to be made in order to be rehoused by the council. If you simply sell your home without telling the local council about your situation you may be considered to have made yourself intentionally homeless. In this case the council might take the view that you have no right to be housed by them.

If you get a letter from your building society showing that you are in arrears, and that they intend to take out a possession order unless your home is sold, than take this straight along to the housing department. It will always help to get things moving there. In practice some councils may insist that they can only help you when formal possession proceedings have commenced. Council policies vary from region to region. Make sure that you understand the legal background and local position exactly.

If there is a Citizens Advice Bureau near you, they might well be able to confirm the local council policy to you, should you feel you have not been given all the information properly. It would certainly be well worth your while to give them a ring or pay them a visit. If need be, go and see your local councillor and try to enlist his or her help to make sure you are getting fair treatment.

In the event that formal proceedings have already commenced to take possession of your home make sure that you complete the forms that are sent with any Court documents and return them. If you do not wish to lose your home then, come what may, attend the Court. At the hearing explain your problems to the Court.

You may be able to obtain legal aid and be represented by

a solicitor. You can check on this with a solicitor. Or your local Citizens Advice Bureau might be prepared to send someone along with you to speak on your behalf.

In Court you should make an offer to pay off the arrears by instalments. If you make such an offer the Court is likely to grant a suspended possession order, which means if you make the payments offered no further action should be taken against you. However, if you fail to keep to the arrangements, then you may be evicted without a further Court hearing. Therefore make sure you can keep to whatever arrangements are agreed with the Court.

You may find it possible to pay off all the arrears with help from family and friends. In such a case the Court can dismiss the application for a possession order and allow you a fresh start.

If you cannot satisfy them that, given time, you can pay off your arrears the Court has no choice but to grant a possession order. You must then leave the property by the given date; otherwise you can be removed by bailiffs. As explained earlier your home will then be sold over your head.

## Second Mortgages

Sometimes people take out a second mortgage on their home in addition to the first mortgage they took out when they originally bought their house. A whole range of financial institutions are prepared to lend money to householders on the security of a charge on their property.

Think out carefully if you can afford to pay the additional payments. Make no mistake, the lender of a second mortgage can ask for a possession order in just the same way as the lender of the first mortgage. The only difference between the two types of mortgage is that the lender of the first mortgage will be paid first if your house is sold. The lender of the second mortgage will only be paid if there is sufficient money left over. He is thus likely to initiate action sooner should you default at any time.

Treat lenders of a second mortgage in the same way as you

treat the lender of the first mortgage. Make contact with them when problems arise and try to make some agreement with them to deal with arrears. With most second mortgages you will probably have to deal with someone in a distant office. Unlike a building society or bank you may be unable to establish personal sympathetic contact with them. Therefore it is very important to write concise, clear letters. Get someone to assist you with this if you have difficulty. Again, you may find that your local Citizens Advice Bureau may be able to help.

Thousands of people lose their homes because of possession orders each year. It is a very traumatic, upsetting experience; do all you can to avoid it.

You might also try to overcome the problem of a second mortgage by increasing the size of your first mortgage. Ask your building society manager. He just might help. Alternatively, you might try to find a new lender to replace both your first and your second mortgage. Some insurance companies may do this for you. Ring a few insurance brokers and see if they will help. Make sure you check the rate of interest if you get such an opportunity.

**Rate Arrears**
There are two things in this world that cannot be avoided, death and taxation. Rates are a form of local taxation and they must be paid. Unless or until the present system is entirely changed (there is strong talk of this as I write) rates remain practically the only debt for which people can be imprisoned.

If you have problems with your rates you will be dealt with by the local Magistrates Court rather than the County Court. If you fail to keep an agreement made with the Magistrates Court, this may result in spending some time at Her Majesty's pleasure, in prison.

The Magistrates Court is a criminal Court and appearing there can be a very distressing experience, more so than in an ordinary civil Court.

Therefore it is obvious that you must give the highest

priority to paying your rates. Unlike rent arrears the local council cannot write-off any rate arrears. The council is obliged by law to collect them in full and there is no escape from paying them.

If you fall into arrears with your rates, contact your rates department of your local council immediately. They will normally agree to an arrangement whereby you have to clear your existing debt before the next rate demand is due.

You really must make sure that you stick to any agreement that you make, otherwise you may receive a Court summons pretty swiftly. If a Court summons is issued you are normally ordered to make payments by specific dates. Failure to pay on time will mean bailiffs from the Court can come and take goods from your house to be sold. Be warned that goods sold in this way fetch a fraction of what you paid for them, so it is possible to lose your goods and ultimately be sent to prison as well.

You may be entitled to help in paying for your rates. Read Chapter 8 which explains how to claim the proper benefits.

# 3

# HIRE PURCHASE DEBTS, BUYING ON CREDIT AND MONEY LENDERS

**Hire Purchase Debts**

When you buy goods on hire purchase the goods do not belong to you until you have paid for them. You cannot dispose of or sell the goods – that would be fraud. Up until that point they are simply on hire to you. They can be repossessed by the hire purchase company if you fail to make payments. (Some contracts give you the option to include default insurance, for example for illness, but I will assume in this chapter that you are not so protected.)

Technically, once a certain number of instalments has been paid the hire purchase company cannot reclaim goods without a Court order, nor are their representatives allowed to enter your home to take possession of the goods. However, most hire purchase companies will not be interested in repossessing, to their way of thinking, second-hand goods. It should therefore be relatively easy to negotiate a system of lower payments if you fall into difficulties. Notice that this means you will have to pay more interest overall, given that the period of repayments will be extended.

Write to the company involved and explain your problems, at the same time offering a lower repayment. Make sure that your offer more than covers the interest being charged otherwise your debt will grow. When difficulties are likely to be temporary some companies will agree to token repayments till you are in a position to resume normal ones; discussion with the company is the key to sorting out your problem with goodwill.

If you find it impossible to make any further payments at all you may have to consider trying to end the agreement that you made with the company. This will boil down to doing some sort of deal with them, preferable to being taken to Court, with the potential that you finish up declared bankrupt. (In Part Two you will see how *one* Court action can precipitate this disaster.)

To be realistic about what sort of deal might be struck you need to have some idea of the way the company will see the matter. On a contract terminated early, an HP company is entitled under consumer law to recoup some of the interest it would have earned had the hire purchase continued to completion.

If they were going to take you to Court, they would work out the remaining amount of debt they could claim on this basis. The interest chargeable up-to-date, plus the extra portion allowed under this rule, would first be calculated. This would then be added to the original cost of the goods, before deducting whatever payments you had made so far to reach the legal claim figure they could make in Court.

The resulting amount is the early settlement figure they will have in mind before doing any deal with you. However, because it will save them the trouble and expense of going to Court, you may well be able to negotiate a somewhat lower figure. Although you may agree between you that part of the money be raised by sale of the goods, second-hand values tend to be dreadful and, being their legal owner, the HP company controls the sale whether you like the price obtained or not.

Nevertheless – having accepted that you must lose the goods – a deal like this can reduce an HP debt quite substantially overall. The snag is that you probably have to pay the whole of the reduced debt at once to keep out of Court.

From all the above you can see how essential it is to come to some agreement with the hire purchase company about how you intend to pay off your debt. If you do not contact or reply to them, or cannot manage the least burdensome scheme they can accept, the company is likely to take you to Court. Substantial Court costs are then liable to get added to your problems.

The Court may or may not instruct that the company be allowed to repossess the goods in part payment but it will certainly order that you must pay off the debt – probably to a strict schedule. In default of whatever the Court has ordered, the company will be in a position to make you bankrupt if they have to. I have already suggested you look in Part Two to see why you must avoid that at almost any cost.

Some HP companies choose to cut their losses differently by using a debt collector rather than getting too involved in the other means of dealing with debtors outlined above. See page 47 if your debt gets referred.

## Buying On Credit

These days there is a vast variety of means of obtaining credit to buy goods. Most large retail groups offer their own credit systems. The main difference between a credit sale and hire purchase is that goods bought under an ordinary credit scheme belong to you and not the company that loaned you the money to buy the goods. You are in a position to sell any goods bought under a credit sale agreement whenever you wish. Your creditors will only be interested in pursuing you for the amount of money owed. They would not be able to repossess any goods that you bought under a credit sale agreement.

If you are struggling to keep up with your payments under a credit sale agreement, you should consider selling the goods you originally purchased in order to pay off your debts. However, one of the disadvantages of widespread and easily available credit is that it leads to a reduction in the second-hand value of most goods.

A second-hand product usually has to be bought for cash, whereas brand new goods can be bought under "easy" credit terms. Be realistic about the price you would expect to get by selling second-hand goods. Once you have bought a product it becomes second-hand. The very first time you put it to use there will be an immediate sharp drop in its value.

The best way to try and sell second-hand goods is to try to find a member of your own family or a friend who might be prepared to buy the goods. If you explain your financial plight to them you might well receive a sympathetic response and fetch a price for your goods that you would not get elsewhere. If you sell to complete strangers, they will, most likely, be hard-headed bargain hunters, expecting to pay relatively low prices. So make sure you make every effort possible to get the highest price for any goods you might wish to sell.

Otherwise, the rules for dealing with this sort of debt problem, are the same as for hire purchase debts. Contact the creditor, preferably by letter, and try to agree to a lower repayment. Failure to reach an agreement will eventually lead to the matter being dealt with in Court.


## Money Lenders

Whilst there are a large number of reputable money lenders around such as the banks and well established credit companies, there are a great many of the other variety too. All money lenders must be licensed and must comply strictly to the acts of parliament that control these matters.

Some of these less reputable companies try to impose a commission fee for lending you the money in the first place and to apply exorbitantly high rates of interest – more than they are entitled to under consumer protection law. If you find yourself in the unfortunate position of owing money to a company which charges what seems to be an excessive rate of interest, then you should immediately contact your local council and ask to speak with the department responsible for trading standards.

They will look into the matter for you and might decide to take action against the company concerned if it is considered that the law has been broken. Certainly no Court would make an order against you based on excessive rates of interest. However, there is no easy rule to decide if the rate of interest you are being charged is too high. A Court would need to examine all the circumstances involved. When there is a high level of risk a Court might well allow that a fairly steep rate of interest is reasonable. When the risk is smaller the same rate of interest might be considered to be excessive.

Your local Citizens Advice Bureau might be able to advise you on this matter. If not they should be able to put you in touch with a solicitor who can help you. Find out what he will charge first before plunging into added expense. Although all these efforts may bring about a reduction in the interest being charged, remember you still have the loan to repay. (If you are lucky to get help to pay off such a loan and finish it early, a finance house will usually make a charge towards interest they would otherwise have earned – in the same way early settlement of HP works – see page 43. Banks tend to be less stringent about this and, as their rates are usually more favourable anyway, this is an added reason to choose them as your source of borrowing if you can.)

A good clue as to whether you are dealing with a disreputable lender is if you find yourself harassed by *constant* visits from agents of the company. Such visits can be very worrying and upsetting. You should write to the firm concerned asking them to stop making further visits. If you are threatened with physical violence in any way, or feel intimidated by a possible use of force, then contact the police and complain. The police will bring a criminal charge against anyone who has used force against you and will certainly warn off a company who you feel are harassing you by constant visits to your home.

If you feel your debt with a money lending firm has grown beyond all chance of your paying back as fast as they demand, it may be sensible to let them take you to Court. See Chapter 10.

In many of our larger cities there are individuals with criminal backgrounds who prey on the needs of the drug addicts and the desperate people of our society. You will notice they put little or nothing in writing through which they might be traced. They operate using threats and fear.

They lend money to the sort of people who are dependent on the next fix, or on alcohol, or who gamble compulsively, etc. These parasites are completely outside the law and charge gigantic rates of interest.

The best thing to do to get out of the hands of such people immediately is to try and borrow the money from your family, or a friend. If you can clear the basic loan and as much interest as a bank might have charged, such loan sharks quickly look for other "victims". If you simply cannot pay fast enough you can call in the police to help but you may fear that physical violence could be used against you if you do. You will have to make a personal decision about this. At the end of the day you might opt to move to another part of the country altogether and make a fresh start. Certainly money lenders of this sort could not make any claim against you in the Courts. That is why they depend on violence, blackmail, give false addresses for themselves, and the rest.

## Debt Collection Agencies

It is legal for companies to sell off their debts to agencies that specialize in recovering debts. This is usually done at a discount. Thus a company might sell on various debts owed to them totalling a thousand pounds, to a debt collection agency for five hundred pounds. The debt collection agency hopes to make a profit by recovering more than the five hundred pounds they paid for the debts. Alternatively an agent may "take over" the debt on a commission basis. If you find that a debt of yours has been passed over to a debt collection agency you must deal with them accordingly. The change in no way alters the legal facts of your owing the money.

With relatively small debts it is normally quite easy to arrange to make smaller repayments to these agencies. They will be pleased to receive a regular inflow of payments. As explained earlier you pay more in the long run but at least you may solve the immediate problem. Write to the debt collection agency involved immediately you know that they now have charge of your debt. Offer to make a regular payment that you can afford and enclose the first payment.

Normally this will be accepted and no further action will follow it. Ask them to confirm how many such payments will be required to clear the debt.

For larger debts a debt collection agency would be looking for fairly substantial repayments. Otherwise you will find that they will quickly apply to a Court for an order to be brought against you just as the original creditor could have done. Often for a larger debt someone from the agency will make a personal visit to discuss the issue with you. Do not allow yourself to be intimidated if such a visit is made, and again, report the matter to the police if you feel you are being physically threatened.

## Standing As A Guarantor For Someone Else's Credit Agreement

If you agree to act as a guarantor for someone else's credit agreement you are liable to pay the debt if the repayments are not made as agreed. You should be given a copy of the agreement so that you understand exactly what your liabilities will be in the event of default. Do not sign any general agreement, only one for a specific debt. Put a copy with your Will so that in the event of your death your trustees will know it exists. They will have to decide whether your estate should continue to carry the risk or what to do if they have no choice.

Most finance companies do not hesitate to enforce agreements made by guarantors. (They have the same legal claim against you as though you were the person who originally received the credit. It is not possible to change your mind and back out once you have signed the form.) When they do you must deal with the debt as if it were your own because legally speaking it is your debt. You do have the right to sue the person who has defaulted to try and recover the money but he is most unlikely to have any. In any case you are likely to be hesitant to do so since it will most likely be a member of your own family, or a friend or neighbour, that you have stood guarantor for. Frankly unless you can afford to write off the amount and know you would do so if it came to that, it is unwise to act as a guarantor for anyone. The damage to relationships that can follow when things go wrong is never worth the risk otherwise.

If you really feel you are unable to meet the terms of your guarantee because of your own financial circumstances write to the finance company explaining your situation. It will do no harm to throw yourself at their mercy and they just might decide it is not worth enforcing the guarantee you made.


### Court Orders

If you reach the stage whereby you receive a Court summons, read it carefully and make sure that you complete it properly, and return it to the Court.

In most circumstances of personal credit default you will not need to attend the Court in person but can deal with the matter by post. For a fuller explanation of Court procedures, you should read Chapter 10.

Normally you should offer to make some repayment when you receive a summons and set out your means and liabilities. If you find it difficult to complete the form seek the advice of a Citizens Advice Bureau or some responsible person you can trust. The registrar of the Court will decide what scheme of payments you will have to make.

Remember that if you default on any of the payments the Court has ordered, the full machine of bankruptcy can be invoked against you straightaway. Bailiffs will arrive pretty fast. In Part Two the awesome cost of bankruptcy is spelt out. Look there, to see why you dare not treat credit debts lightly.

If you fail to reply to a summons, in the fullness of time you will find bailiffs on your doorstep anyway, demanding payment in full, and having legal authority to take away some, or all, of your possessions in lieu, if you have not got the money.

Understand that if your goods are taken and sold, usually for a fraction of what you paid for them, you will still be responsible for the balance of the debt. The bailiffs may return if they think you have enough they can reasonably seize but if your debt is clearly too large you can be made bankrupt.

# 4

# BANK OVERDRAFTS AND PERSONAL LOANS, AND CREDIT CARDS

Banks are the largest lending institutions in our society. A majority of the population have an account with them and many millions of people have debts with their banks of one sort or another.

The major high street clearing banks are loth in the extreme to enforce Court actions against their customers. They tend to see bad local publicity, even when their action may be fair, as against their own interests. They prefer to accept reasonable arrangements with their customers to deal with debt problems.

If you are worried by debt problems that have built up with your bank make an appointment to see the manager and lay your cards on the table. Explain your circumstances fully and honestly. Most banks will go out of their way to try to solve your problems with you if you do this. Banking in Britain is still done on a very personal basis. Most bankers are human, they often have problems of their own, and they are usually very easy to talk to.

Let the bank suggest what is to be done for you. At the end of the day banks want their money back like any other lender but they do try to be reasonable.

Do not hide anything from your bank and make sure any promises you make will not be broken. Otherwise they will cease to trust you. Our banking system is based on trust. Break that trust and you will find that you have problems. Possibly you have been telling white lies to the bank about mythical forthcoming promotions or the like in order to obtain further credit. Come clean about everything. A bank will always respect your honesty even if they do not like hearing what you have to say.

The worst thing you can do is to ignore any letters or warnings you receive from your bank. If you continue that way for any length of time you will eventually be "disowned" by your local branch. This means all the details of your debts will be sent to the section of the head office which is responsible for legal actions. They will move somewhat impersonally and fast.

It is far better to have things dealt with at the local level because you are much more likely to receive sympathy and support. Lean on the shoulder of your local bank manager. Cry on his shoulder if you have to. In larger branches you may be dealing with an assistant manager or some other official. Their shoulders will do just as well. The assistant manager of a large branch could well have more authority than the manager of a small branch.

Sometimes the personal nature of our banking system can work against customers. A bank manager may be of the sort who is over-generous and accommodating in making loans to customers. The snag is that very often managers of this kind are moved on after a year or so, or transferred to some other department. Customers then find themselves faced with a new regime of "tight-fistedness" because a new manager has been moved in to rectify a too lax lending policy. An unduly nervous replacement for a perfectly good manager – a one-ulcer man suddenly pitched into a two-ulcer position – may equally expect to apply tougher terms, even on long established customers.

Borrowers in a weak position because they are unable to pay off their loans straightaway can find themselves more than a little disconcerted by the sudden change. Where once they were welcomed by a friendly smile and a wave into the manager's office they now find themselves under the glare of a grim-faced newcomer.

Where lending has been excessive the new manager is almost certainly under strict instructions to bring the lending of that particular branch under control. His grim attitude on the surface is his defence and armour to protect himself for the difficult job he has to do. Try to win him over by your good humour and honesty. If this fails plan to change your bank as soon as you can clear anything you owe.

In some cases there is a straightforward clash of personalities between bankers and their customers. You know yourself it is impossible to like everyone. Sometimes you take an instant liking to a person and at other times the reverse. If you feel ill-at-ease talking to your banker, again consider changing your bank. It is much easier to talk to someone you like and feel you can get on with.

Another bank might not necessarily welcome you with open arms along with your large overdraft. They might shut the door firmly in your face. But another bank may be prepared to help you and it is certainly worth a try. Sales people say that if you do not knock on doors you will never make sales. Who knows, with a different set-up, you may find a manager willing to arrange an overdraft facility or a personal loan at a keener rate of interest, never mind being more accommodating generally?

You do not necessarily have to transfer your debts from one bank to another. You can leave your existing debts with your present bank and simply open a new account with another bank. Many people, especially businessmen, have several bank accounts with different banks. This enables you to develop a hopefully friendly relationship with your new bank while you deal in a more formal manner with the problems of the debt with your other bank.

Thus, there is some scope for flexibility in dealing with debt problems with banks and you should always have an eye for the various options open to you.

**Overdrafts**

An overdraft allows you to overdraw on your current account up to an agreed limit. An overdraft is very flexible. You do not need to use the full facility and interest is only charged on the actual money that is borrowed. An overdraft is normally the cheapest form of bank borrowing because interest charged is only a few per cent higher than the bank's base rate. Although base rates can shoot up (or down) alarmingly, total borrowing cost on an overdraft is almost always cheaper by a wide margin against the real Annual Percentage Rate (APR) price of a fixed repayment loan. An APR rate of interest for a bank loan can be as much as 7 or 8 percentage points higher than an overdraft rate, depending on customer status.

The disadvantages of an overdraft are that you may well have to pay bank charges for servicing the account whilst it is overdrawn, and that there may be an arrangement facility fee to pay (usually only on large overdrafts and at the manager's discretion). It is also true that, legally they are *repayable on demand* (unless special arrangements have been made) although with an arranged limit *in writing*, a bank should be unlikely to be too heavy handed.

The fact that a bank may be able to call in an overdraft at a moment's notice, combined with the fact that to write a cheque you know will bounce is fraud, results in a grey area about which you ~ ust be careful. The system can give the bank a powerful hold over you, more so if you do not get written confirmation of any agreed overdraft facility.

The area becomes "grey" because sometimes a bank will allow an overdraft to build up even if no agreement has formally been made about one. If you have been a regular customer for a number of years many banks will allow a modest overdraft to develop a bit like this before they want to speak to you about it. Once you are into overdraft, technically the bank could refuse to honour a cheque you have written. Few would do so without giving you the opportunity to sort matters out but mistakes happen and the damage to your credit rating via whoever you intended to pay can spread wide.

The right way to go about having an overdraft is to have a formal limit to it set before you get into the red, and to have an agreed "rate over base rate". Not surprisingly most banks hike up the rate a couple of points or so extra on *unarranged* overdrafts, so it is stupid not to sort things out before you need to borrow.

However your overdraft has arisen, you will need to make arrangements to deal with it if it becomes a problem to you. The best way is to arrange your financial affairs so that the overdraft gradually reduces itself. As long as your bank can see that your overdraft is being brought under control they are unlikely to cause you any problems. Bankers are usually happy to see overdrafts which are at least substantially cleared from time to time. Large deficits which drag on for more than a few months attract their close attention, naturally.

If the situation has reached the point where the bank is sending you warning letters, you need to see your bank manager immediately. The manager could soon decide to bounce your cheques otherwise.

Sometimes a bank will suggest you pay off an overdraft which they are unwilling to continue by converting the debt into a bank loan. You have little choice unless you can find a banker prepared to compete and offer you a better deal. This means that although you will be paying a far higher rate of interest, you can at least solve your problem and repay the debt over a longer period of time. A possible advantage is that you may then save on bank charges so long as you keep your current account in credit. Many overdraft problems are dealt with in this way.


**Bank Personal Loan**

A bank personal loan is money borrowed for a particular purpose, for example to buy a car. The loan is kept as a separate account with the bank and you are required to pay it off in regular instalments over an agreed period. This period is usually not more than five years. The rate of interest is most often fixed at the time the loan is taken out, although some are made variable according to changing rates of interest.

If you fall behind with these payments the bank will usually agree for you to make increased payments in the future which enable you to catch up with the arrears. So long as the bank gets back the loan it gave you and the interest within the agreed period there should be little difficulty in arranging a revised schedule of repayments.

The bank may offer to reschedule the loan by your taking out a new loan to pay the old one. This is like borrowing from Peter to pay Paul but it has the advantage of enabling you to repay your debt over a longer period. Ask your bank if they would be willing to do this for you. You might be able to fix a lower rate of interest too. The total cost of the loan is nevertheless likely to rise because of the increased length of time the bank is lending it to you. On the subject of total cost you should always look at the Annual Percentage Rate (APR) being quoted. APRs are calculated according to a government set formula so that they are always strictly comparable and you can therefore work out the true cost of buying on credit from one source as against another.

## Credit Cards

All the major banks now have their own or a shared credit card system. If you settle your monthly bank credit card account by the specified date you will pay no interest. If you cannot or do not wish to pay the full amount your statement will show a minimum payment that you are expected to make. A rate of interest per month which will vary depending on the bank's base rate will be charged on the balance outstanding. In Annual Percentage Rate (APR) terms this rate is enormously high, making the cost of getting credit this way uncompetitive except for the convenience.

It is very easy to build up debts quickly with credit cards partly because handing over a plastic card to buy goods never hurts in quite the same way as handing over hard cash. If you find your credit card debts out of control take a pair of scissors and cut your card into pieces. This way, you will at least not add any further debts to your problems.

A limit is set by arrangement with your local branch on the amount of money you can spend when you first take out a credit card from a bank. Later on however, should you reach the specified limit the quite separate credit card division of your bank usually just increases the existing limit for you without your asking. They simply write and tell you what your new limit is. In this way, and because they sometimes raise everybody's limits with inflation or maybe to encourage business, your own limit can go much too high for your own good before they might put the brakes on. Therefore you need to keep a very close control on what you are spending.

If your credit card debts get out of control it is no use turning to your local bank manager. As explained credit cards are issued by special sections of the major banks which are independently managed. You need to write directly to the address on your credit card statement explaining the difficulties you are having, and describing your circumstances.

You may then be able to arrange a system of repayments whereby your debts are eventually repaid. A condition of such an arrangement will almost certainly be that you make no further use of your card. Lack of action by you over a credit card problem, or inability to pay even with a specially agreed slower rate, will lead to Court like any other debt. As that can trigger bankruptcy proceedings (see end of this Chapter, and Part Two) you must spare no effort to prevent it.

## Personal Loans Through Your Bank Credit Card

The so-called "privilege" of having a bank credit card brings glowing invitations which "entitle" you to borrow at "special rates" from the credit card company. (We have noted above that they are a separate entity from the bank.) For all practical purposes such a loan is exactly the same as an ordinary bank loan. The main difference, which may pay for the tempting advertising, is that the interest rate will be a point or two higher . . . Problems that arise should be dealt with as advised earlier in this Chapter.

## When A Bank Turns Nasty

You may have reached the situation where your bank are

sending you thoroughly unpleasant letters warning you that they intend to take legal action to recover their debts. This can be extremely frightening and usually it indicates a complete breakdown in normal relations between you and your bank. If you only make contact with your local branch at this late stage you may well be informed that the matter is already out of their hands and is being dealt with by the legal department of their head office.

Even at this point it will be worth trying to come to terms with your bank branch, despite the fact that you may receive an extremely icy reception at first. It will at least show the bank that you are anxious to find a solution, even if they are not in a position to call off the attentions of head office.

Should your affairs be handed over to the bank's legal section, you are at once in a different ball game. You need to adopt alternative tactics. It will no longer be possible to make the personal approach that was available to you while your affairs were in the hands of the local branch. As soon as you receive the first letter from the legal section of the bank, you should write to them immediately explaining that you are extremely concerned and want to reach a solution to your problems. Make your own suggestions about how you intend to repay the money. After a few days follow the matter through by making a telephone call and asking to discuss the best way forward.

Banks always try to avoid legal action against their customers. As a result they will invariably treat people who are clearly trying their best to deal with their debt problems sympathetically.

You may be able to do some "horse trading" with the bank. For example, say you owe the bank five thousand pounds. Very often a large part of this debt will consist of accrued interest and only a small part will be the original capital borrowed. If you can find a member of your family, or a friend, prepared to make an offer of say, three thousand five hundred pounds to the bank in exchange for the bank writing the balance off, you may well find that you can do business.

This is particularly the case if you can demonstrate to the bank that you are worthy of special sympathy because of your own circumstances. Banks do tend to make "moral" judgments about their customers and treat them accordingly. So it is certainly well worth making an effort to do a deal with the bank if you possibly can.

However, at the end of the day, if you cannot reach an agreement with the bank you will be faced with Court proceedings. If so you should read Chapter 10.

In some cases a Court order can work to your advantage because once your debt is the subject of a Court order, further interest might not be added to your debt unless your creditor makes a further application to the Court. However if the debt is very large and you have assets, the bank might well opt to press a bankruptcy notice against you. As Part Two shows, the effects of a bankruptcy can be disastrous. Take every measure possible to avoid getting anywhere near it. If you once get into bankruptcy proceedings it is quite common for a good half of your assets to be lost in the process itself as it grinds remorselessly against you. That really hurts when you add it to what you owe all around. It makes it virtually certain that your last penny will indeed go.

# 5

# ELECTRICITY, GAS AND TELEPHONE ARREARS

Major sources of debt and worry for many people are their fuel bills. Particularly during periods of cold weather very large bills can quickly develop. Often it is the elderly and the less well-off who are at home all day, with the consequent need to keep their homes warm most of the time, who have the biggest bills.

Huge increases in the cost of electricity and gas in the last few years have caused problems for many more people than before. If you do not pay a gas or electricity board, your fuel supplies can be cut off without the need to obtain a Court order. Gas and electricity officials have the right of entry to your home to cut you off if you have not paid a bill. But they must have a warrant to do this. They can also take you to Court later to obtain payment of money already owed. And there is a fat charge for being reconnected.

Therefore, it is essential that you contact your local electricity or gas board immediately if you find you are unable to pay your latest bill. Do not delay in doing this. Take action as soon as you realise you cannot pay all, or part of the account.

Make an offer that you can afford so as to pay off the arrears say, on a fortnightly basis. Remember to allow for the fact that you will continue to use gas and electricity and that there will soon be another bill. Do not make an offer that you may be unable to keep to. It is better to offer a smaller payment knowing you will easily maintain it. You can write or telephone to make such an offer, or you can go in person to the local office. Someone else can also do it for you if there is any reason you cannot get on with it yourself straightaway.

There are several ways in which the strain of a large quarterly bill can be avoided. Stamps can be purchased and there are various easy-payment schemes whereby you can make regular payments in advance to meet your bills. Ask at your local electricity or gas board. If you are the sort who cannot save, start one of these methods.

If you find that you cannot reach an agreement on the repayment of such a debt, you can ask for a pre-payment "slot" meter to be installed which will be set to recover some of the debt from every coin you put into the meter. The big advantage of this is that you will no longer have to face future quarterly bills and you can monitor on a daily basis the amount of fuel you are using. It can be a great aid to imposing "fuel discipline". The meter can be re-set once the debt is cleared.

### Reducing Your Fuel Bills

Your fuel bills may be persistently higher than you expect. Possibly your meter is not operating properly. You can ask for your meter to be checked by your local gas or electricity board. You should do this if you cannot think of an explanation as to why your bills are so high. If your meter is not operating correctly you will be entitled to a refund. However, it is very rare for a meter not to be working properly. If your fuel bills are very high it is much more likely that you are wasting fuel in several ways and you can put this right by a number of methods.

### Cutting Down On Electricity

Sheer carelessness can cost you dearly. Make sure you always switch off a light when you leave a room. Check on your bulb sizes. Do not just stick any old bulb in a socket when it needs replacing. Bathroom, bedroom and landing lights need only be small. The places where you really need a more powerful light are in your main living room and in the kitchen for safety.

It is surprising how much money can be saved by paying attention to such simple points. People who really think carefully about using electricity can cut down their fuel bills considerably.

Immersion heaters are wasteful users of electricity. If you have an immersion heater installed to heat your water, you should treat it as enemy number one. Firstly, check that the hot water cylinder is properly lagged. It does not cost much to have this done and it saves the money spent within a few weeks. Secondly check that the thermostat is not set too high and that it is working properly. Thermostats sometimes break down and this can run away with electricity.

See if the electricity board is running any schemes whereby you can obtain cheap rate electricity, by heating your water at night, for example. Consider whether some alternative form of heating water such as gas would be cheaper.

Other major users of electricity are electric fires. Again, consider switching to some other form of heating. The capital outlay can repay its cost surprisingly quickly.

## Cutting Down On Gas

Some gas appliances are more efficient than others. It could be well worth obtaining the advice of your local gas board regarding the type of gas installations you are using. In particular, there are gas water heaters which only use fuel when water is actually drawn from the tap. Some gas fires have their own thermostats which control the use of fuel and help you economise. As with electric heating it can be well worth your while to invest some money if it will produce big savings on bills. Often it is possible to buy gas appliances and pay for them by instalments on your quarterly bill, or even through a pre-payments "slot" meter.

## What To Do If You Get Cut Off

If you cannot pay your fuel bill and make no arrangements to pay off the arrears your fuel supplies will be cut off. Gas and electricity officials have the right of entry to your home for this purpose if they have obtained a warrant. These boards will not hesitate to cut off supplies especially where a bill is very large and their demands go unanswered.

If your supply is about to be cut off (or has been) contact your local Social Services Department and the local DHSS office immediately to see if they will help you. Between them they should know exactly to what help you may be entitled if any, and how to make sure the board in question deals with you accordingly. Ask at your local Town Hall for the address of the Social Services Department.

Before a supply will be reconnected you have to make some sort of arrangement to pay off arrears and you may have to pay a deposit as well as a reconnection charge. If you have been on a quarterly bill system and you ask to have a pre-payment "slot" meter installed the deposit is sometimes reduced.

**Purchasing Gas And Electricity From A Landlord**
If you live in rented accommodation then you might well be purchasing your supplies from your landlord. Each gas and electricity board lays down a maximum price that may be charged for the re-sale of gas and electricity. A tenant can recover from the landlord any amount by which the landlord has overcharged. If you suspect you are being overcharged check with the respective board.

If your landlord collects your meter money but then does not pay the fuel bill, contact your local council. They have the power to pay your fuel bill and then collect the money from your landlord. This will ensure that your fuel supply will not be cut off.

**Telephone Bills**
Telephone bills can be a major source of worry. If you are in debt you should consider getting rid of your telephone altogether to cut down on your expenses.

You may, however, have a number of reasons that make it essential for you to have a telephone. In this case it is important to keep outgoing calls to a minimum. If you must make a call keep it short and if at all possible make it during the cheap rate period.

If you cannot pay your present bill you can usually make arrangements with British Telecom to pay off your arrears by instalments so long as this is done over a reasonable period. You can arrange to pay future bills by buying telephone stamps or making a standing order for monthly amounts.

## An Unusually Large Telephone Bill

People are sometimes horrified to receive an exceptionally large bill. There can be several reasons for this, but it is rarely faulty machinery at the telephone exchange. More often it is closer to home. Teenage children are notorious wasters of their parents' money when using the telephone! The baby-sitter may have a boy-friend in the Antipodes! It may be necessary for you to obtain a telephone lock so that only you can use the telephone. Telephone locks can be obtained at a Telecom showroom.

You can also arrange to have your telephone disconnected for the purpose of outgoing calls and simply pay the standard rental to receive incoming calls.

If however, you remain convinced that your household is not responsible for the large bill you have received then you should complain strongly to British Telecom. They will probably monitor your calls for a while to see if the high usage is continuing. They will also check their call charging equipment. Usually they will insist they are right and you will have to pay the bill although they may allow you to do this by instalments.

Customers who stick to their ground and insist they are not responsible for the high bill, and whose normal calls are found by the monitoring to run at a lesser rate, can usually negotiate an agreement for a reduction to be made in the bill.

## If You Are Disconnected

Do not simply ignore a telephone bill even if you cannot pay it. If you do this you will be disconnected and will have to pay a heavy fee to be reconnected in addition to the bill you owe. So make contact with British Telecom and come to some agreement about how you intend to pay the bill. They are very unlikely to cut you off if you have made arrangements with them.

# 6

# DIVORCE, MAINTENANCE PAYMENTS AND THE SINGLE PARENT

**Divorce**

This Chapter is concerned solely with dealing with debt problems that arise through divorce and not with the wider legal, and family matters. Getting divorced is a very traumatic, emotional experience in most cases. Difficult financial problems can add to the hurt. It is only too easy to arrive at a stalemate when decisions need to be reached over dividing the property, making arrangements regarding the children, and agreeing on possible maintenance payments. Even if your divorce is not specially problematical you may need specialist advice, and it is sensible to increase your own knowledge of the subject by looking through some of the books written specifically in order to help you.

Major conflicts will be settled by the divorce Courts. Unless they are satisfied you have made a responsible agreement they will decide how the property is to be divided, and on the level of maintenance payments. However, although they may take into consideration what you tell them about existing debts, it is not always possible for them to allow adequately for all eventualities.

For example, a married couple might have debts in their joint names. A creditor can call on both of them to repay that debt. Failing that, he can call on either one for whatever remains unpaid. The best way to explain your legal responsibilities in this regard is to take a typical case.

Alan and Kay have just been divorced after ten years of marriage. Alan had credit card debts in his own name of twelve hundred pounds. Kay had taken out a hire purchase agreement in her own name for three hundred pounds to purchase some furniture. In addition, they had a joint bank account which had an overdraft of nine hundred pounds.

While they were married they had been pooling their finances and jointly paying off their various debts. However, once the divorce took place, they each took to their own corners. Alan was legally responsible for paying his credit card debts. No claim could be made against Kay for them. In the same way, Kay was responsible for the hire purchase debt she incurred, and no claim could be made against Alan by the HP company.

However, both Kay and Alan were responsible for repaying the overdraft to the bank. Alan felt that because he had such large credit card debts and as they were both working and earning similar wages, that Kay should be responsible for paying off the bank. He angrily demanded this but she refused and Alan failed to pay off any of it either.

The position portrayed so far is by no means unusual. In the end one of them will probably get lumbered with the whole bill. Let us see how this can happen.

Suppose Alan, to escape paying the debt, chooses to leave the country. Kay will then be responsible for paying off the whole of the overdraft. A Court order instigated by the bank will be binding upon her. The same would be true of Alan in the reverse position but that is no consolation if you are the injured party!

Alternatively imagine the position after the divorce were Kay to be the only one with a job and appreciable money coming in. The bank would soon tire of chasing Alan and would take Kay to Court for the lot.

You can see from Alan and Kay's story how vital it is to make some friendly agreement with your ex-spouse about joint debts. Ignoring the problem or choosing to be stubborn can only cause problems. Even if the divorce Court had been able to foresee such an end result it did not have any authority which could change the legal fact that, whilst both parties were liable for the debt, one of them could be made to pay it off alone.

Divorce often brings an increase in debt burdens. Instead of one household, two have to be maintained. Anyone considering divorce should think carefully about the financial implications and seek to come to an agreement with the other party about how any additional debt is to be shared out.

It is very common for couples to neglect the financial aspects of their marriage when emotional problems begin to cause a rift. This neglect of basic finances sometimes makes the emotional problems worse. (It can even be the neglect of family finances that directly leads to divorce.) Hard to cope with as your emotional difficulties may be, you should always keep a careful eye on your financial affairs and at least try to work together on them.

## Maintenance Payments

The level of any maintenance payments may be arranged by a Magistrates Court, or by a divorce Court. Both Courts have similar powers to order maintenance payments to be made. The amount will depend upon all the individual circumstances. It can also be increased or decreased if the position changes in the future. Reapply to the Court if you need an adjustment.

Like the non-payment of rates, the failure to make court-ordered maintenance payments is one of the few debts that can lead to eventual imprisonment. Nearly always it is the man who has to make maintenance payments to his ex-wife. Thousands of men have been committed to prison for falling into arrears on these payments. Therefore, if you have a maintenance order against you, treat this extremely seriously.

Magistrate's clerks will not usually recommend summonses for arrears of maintenance until they have built up to a considerable sum. So do not think you are going to get away with not paying maintenance, or not paying all of it, just because you are not immediately served with a summons. You can be sure that if your ex-spouse presses for it a summons will eventually be served.

When this happens you will have to appear in Court to explain why you have not paid or paid fully. If you can show you have a good reason for not paying, the Court can reduce the amount of maintenance to be paid in future. For example, you may have become unemployed, or you may have remarried giving you additional financial responsibilities. In most cases, however, the original award will stand and you will be told to pay up promptly and fully, henceforward. The Court will also instruct you in regard to the arrears outstanding. Although arrears stretching back beyond twelve months are occasionally written off or reduced, the usual thing is to be made to pay off *all* such arrears of maintenance by instalments, keeping up with your usual payments at the same time. The Court will normally back up these decisions by threatening an attachment of earnings order, or even imprisonment.

If you have a steady job and an attachment of earnings order is made, your employer will have to deduct the maintenance payments from your wages. Having your employer made aware of the fact that you have a Court order against you can damage your prospects, human nature being as it is. Avoid it happening if you possibly can but if it does, be sure to keep your employer informed ahead of events.

If the Court decides that you have deliberately and wilfully failed to pay maintenance you can be sent to prison. However, prison is the last resort, unusual except against someone who unreasonably and persistently fails to make payments and where an attachment of earnings order would not be appropriate.

If a prison sentence is passed it will usually be for a few weeks. Or you might receive a suspended sentence. This means you will only be sent to prison if you fail to make the payments the Court orders. This is your last chance to save yourself from imprisonment. If you are put in jail you will still be responsible for paying any arrears, although sometimes the Court will give you a fresh start by cancelling the existing debt. You will, however, have to make the usual payments in the future.

Should your ex-wife remarry you will no longer have to

make maintenance payments for her. However, any maintenance order made in respect of children will have to be paid until the children are 16, and in some cases 18, even if your ex-wife does remarry. Maintenance orders can be rescinded if you resume normal marital relationships with your wife for a period of more than six months. In this case, both husband and wife should sign a letter to the Court stating that they have been cohabiting together for six months and that they wish the maintenance arrangements to be ended.

## The Single Parent

Maybe as a result of being divorced or perhaps because your partner has died, you fall into the category of being a single parent with the sole responsibility of bringing up your children. Father or mother, special payments are available to you, outlined in Chapter 8.

On the question of maintenance some single parents, for emotional reasons, decide not to pursue their claims officially and run into financial problems as a result. If you believe you are entitled to maintenance do make sure you pursue it and that you are not merely, at great hardship to yourself, subsidising your ex-spouse by not doing so.

It is nearly always women who claim maintenance from their ex-husbands but when a man is left with the children there is nothing to stop him claiming maintenance from his ex-wife. It is very easy to apply for a maintenance order in a Magistrates Court. There is no need to use a solicitor unless very large sums of money are likely to be involved. Simply telephone or call in at the office of the clerk to the magistrates. The address can be obtained from your local telephone book, or from a Citizens Advice Bureau.

You will have to fill out a form and make a brief appearance before the local magistrate, who will ask a few questions. A summons will then be issued against the other party to appear in Court.

Maintenance hearings are domestic matters and are held in private so do not worry about any of the details spreading by gossip.

You will both be asked about your general family and financial circumstances. It helps to take along with you any evidence you might have such as rent books, mortgage agreements, details of hire purchase debts, etc.

If maintenance awarded to you is not being paid properly you must go back to the court. You should also approach the DHSS who may be able to assist you meanwhile.

# 7

# HOW TO NEGOTIATE
# WITH CREDITORS

1. Always make contact with the people you owe money to.
2. Never ignore any letters or demands from them.
3. Make out a precise statement of your income and expenditure as in Chapter 1, so that you can make sure you offer to reduce each debt as much as you can, (also see below).
4. Try to make a game out of it if this will help you not to get upset, or worry too much because you owe money. Undue anxiety will not assist you or your creditors.

The telephone is not suitable for making arrangements for dealing with debt problems, except in an emergency. Messages get lost, and two people talking together on the telephone often have a very different view of what they agreed to. Put everything in writing and keep copies. If you do phone, then confirm what is agreed by letter the same day.

Your letters should be brief and clear. Bear in mind that creditors are not interested in hearing of your life history or the long chain of events that have led you to your having to write. They really just want to know how you intend to repay them. Most creditors will look more favourably on your predicament if they hear from you before payments fall behind rather than when they have already had to chase you.

**Examples Of Letters To Creditors**

1. You have just lost your job.

Your address

Date

Creditor's name and address

Dear Sir

AGREEMENT/ACCOUNT NO....................

I write to inform you that I was made redundant last month.

I had only worked for the firm for eighteen months so I am not entitled to any redundancy pay. My only income now is the social security money to which I am entitled of £XX per week for me, my wife and my three children.

I have carefully worked out what I need to cover my basic living expenses and find that I can only afford to pay £5 a month on our agreement.

Would you please be kind enough to help me, by accepting this reduced payment until I manage to find another job?

Yours faithfully

Your name

Make your letter legible and remember to put the date, your name and address, and the agreement number at the top. It is surprising how many debtors send off letters with basic information missing, making it harder for a creditor to deal properly with them.

If interest is being charged on your debt (e.g. credit cards, bank overdrafts, etc) also ask that the interest be frozen for the time being, otherwise you can find the debt still rising despite the payments you are able to make. Never be afraid to request this extra sort of temporary help whilst you genuinely need it (see page 74).

2. Here is an example of the letters you might write if you

have an income but owe money to several creditors. Total repayments are too big to handle but the problem is not sufficiently pressing to warrant asking for suspension of the interest.

Your address

Date

Creditor's name and address

Dear Sir

AGREEMENT/ACCOUNT NO....................

I refer to the repayment schedule of our agreement above...... (or, if you have already a complaint from them, "I refer to your letter/payment demand dated –/–/–)... and wish to explain my financial circumstances.

I earn £XXX per week and have to support two young children and my wife, who is unable to work while the children are still aged 18 months and 6 weeks respectively. My only other income is £XX in child benefit each week.

I attach a list showing my present weekly/monthly commitments. You will see from it that I have only £XX left to divide amongst my creditors and that my other expenses are already pared to the bone. My repayments began to run higher than I could manage before I took a close enough look at the total position and I now appreciate the necessity for getting back into balance with my affordable income.

In order to hold the line I am sure you will appreciate that all I can afford to do is offer to pay 20% less on each of the regular repayments concerned. Hence I am writing similarly to each of my creditors. I will be grateful if you are able to reduce your rate accordingly, with an appropriate alteration to the date that the last payment will become due. Confirmation of such revised terms, so that I can see the new finishing date, would be helpful.

I am sorry that this problem has arisen, and should there be any change in my circumstances enabling me to resume the original rate, I will inform you immediately.

Please let me know if you will agree to this offer.

Yours faithfully

Your name

Do not fall into the tempting trap of paying off some of your smaller creditors altogether and ignoring the others for the time being. It is not your small creditors that are likely to cause you the most trouble but your larger ones. Pay some money to all your creditors, to try to keep them happy. By paying even a very small amount to each creditor at least they know that you are trying to do something about your debt.

Generally speaking pay the most to the largest creditor. However, be prepared to adopt a degree of self-preservation strategy.

Consider this example. Mr Jones has the following debts.

| | | |
|---|---|---|
| Credit card | £700 | (At 23% interest per annum) |
| Hire purchase | £800 | (At 27% interest per annum) |
| Rent arrears | £950 | (No interest being added) |

Mr Jones writes to the credit card company and the hire purchase company asking them to freeze any interest charges. The hire purchase company refuses but the credit card company agrees for twelve months. No interest is being added to the £950 rent arrears.

The strategy here would be to pay sufficient money to the credit card company and your landlord to keep them happy, and to pay off the largest amount of money on the hire purchase debt, which is the only one carrying interest.

A calculator and/or a friend who is good at maths can be a

boon to help you work out the best plan. It is vital to keep in constant touch with your creditors so you can be flexible if one starts to get nervous.

Dealing with your debts in this way can turn into a very interesting game. A constant nagging worry can transform into a sense of enjoyment and achievement. So long as your debts are being reduced by even the smallest amount, you are getting somewhere. Remember how long it took to build the pyramids. Do not give up, or lose heart.

## Borrowing From Peter To Pay Paul

There are times when it does make sense to borrow from Peter to pay Paul. Be warned to ignore starry-eyed loan advertisements. Only a friendly Peter will be the slightest use. Someone in your family circle, perhaps parents, might be prepared to help, or you might be lucky enough to have the proverbial wealthy aunt. Apart from this, or help by your bank discussed below, it is very unlikely you will be able to replace one set of debts with another – except at vastly higher rates of interest likely to lead you into a life of long-term penury.

If a member of your family is prepared to replace a debt bearing interest with a debt bearing no interest at all, swallow your pride and accept.

Remember though, to give special attention to paying such a family debt back. Messing around quickly leads to strained relationships. Nonetheless, if you are setting out to deal with your debt problems in a concerned and responsible way, it is not unreasonable of you to ask for, and accept help from members of your family. Sometimes it will be a close friend who helps you over a difficult period. Be absolutely frank. Do not make promises you cannot keep, or paint a falsely rosy picture. Friends and family are worth far more than gold so always be honest in your dealings with them.

If you have not already asked you may be surprised at the degree of help your bank can give. If you must owe money to any financial institution your local bank is usually the best place. A bank will want its pound of flesh but is likely to be the most flexible of creditors to deal with. The interest you pay should be at one of the most reasonable market rates available. A straightforward overdraft to replace a set of high interest bearing debts would be the cheapest (see page 52) but you may have to settle for a single bank loan at a favourable rate of interest. For example if you have various credit card debts at high rates of interest, it would be perfectly sensible and reasonable to ask your bank for a loan to pay off those debts.

If they agree, then destroy those credit cards. There is no better way to bring such debts under control.

However, do not expect your bank manager to give you a loan to cover large debts which you have run up irresponsibly. You will receive a very cold reception. He is quite likely to show you the door rapidly. Present him with a realistic, sensible proposition that takes into account all your financial circumstances. If you think your bank manager is being unreasonable or unhelpful, changing banks may be a possibility – see page 52.

**Dealing With Awkward Creditors**
You can be sure that whether you have five or twenty creditors, some will prove extremely awkward, putting on the greatest pressure. If you can pay such strident creditors first, do. It is not worth the hassle of constantly clashing swords with them. It is far better to deal with a large number of friendly and helpful creditors than a small number of unfriendly ones. It is probably best just to accept that the awkward squad are of the sort who deliberately adopt a policy of constant harassment, knowing that they are thus likely to be paid promptly.

Their pressure can be by way of constant threatening letters or telephone calls. Worst of all though, is the personal call with the knock at the door always arriving as you are in the middle of entertaining friends or relatives. Do not allow yourself to feel or be physically intimidated. If you feel frightened in any way make a complaint to the police. This will put an end to any further visitors in the vast majority of cases.

**Telephoning Creditors**

The importance of writing to creditors has already been stressed. However, if a creditor sends an unhelpful reply to your written letter, it can pay to make a more personal approach by telephone. Make sure that you are talking to the right person. It is of little use telephoning a large financial institution and talking to a raw new recruit. Find out the name of the person who can make decisions about your affairs and talk to him or her.

Always be polite and show you are concerned about the problem however discourteous the person to whom you are talking may be. Do not be tempted to respond angrily to any harsh words that may be spoken. Bite your tongue, or you will only set back your cause. Explain that you have written to them but they proved unhelpful. Go over your problems briefly again and ask if they will reconsider their position.

Follow up the telephone call with a further letter, stressing the points you made on the telephone. Even the most difficult of creditors may revise their approach once they recognise how serious you are about dealing with your debt.

**Personal Visits To Your Creditors**

Sometimes it will pay off to make a personal visit to your creditor. This would apply especially where you know the person concerned, for example your builder. A direct visit to explain your problem is clear proof to them of your seriousness and integrity. A creditor who may have been planning to serve you with a Court writ might well adopt a more charitable approach as a result. All creditors want their money but they are human too, and a frank and clear explanation why you cannot pay all your bills on time might well draw their sympathy.

Unless distance and cost are prohibitive nothing is lost by such a visit. You can only stand to gain. Even if you find you meet with an angry reception, when you have left you can be sure your creditor will rethink his attitude towards you.

# 8

# CLAIMING YOUR PROPER BENEFITS

Benefits by nature depend on political whim. New ones are forever being dreamed up. Others get cut. Constant changes in practical procedure and qualifying rules seem inevitable as do wide variations in their interpretation. As I write a root and branch review of the entire system is in progress. This Chapter would become a book in itself were I to describe the literally thousands of types of help available. It would also be out of date before the printing ink was dry. So I will concentrate on how you track down and claim all those individual benefits to which you may be entitled.

Millions of pounds go unclaimed each year and I believe one result is large numbers of people with debt problems, which could have been avoided had they been claiming their proper benefits. As you may never have heard of some of the benefits that exist you must search every avenue. Examples range from home help to extra cash for looking after an orphaned child unofficially. Do not be afraid to look just because you think your income may not be low enough to be included. Earnings are not always taken into account anyway. When they are, you can find exclusion is at a much higher level than you might have thought.

**Getting The Facts**
Start to work your way through the vast maze by obtaining from the local Department of Health and Social Security the latest edition of the free guide called "Which Benefit?" reference FB2. This will guide you to all the other specific

DHSS benefit leaflets there are, and it even includes an order form for them. Call back and get copies of every leaflet which could remotely apply to you. If you have any difficulty in obtaining what you want at your local office, short-circuit the local inertia and write directly to: DHSS Leaflets, Canons Park, Government Buildings, PO Box 21, Honeypot Lane, Stanmore, Middlesex, HA7 1AY, stating the titles of leaflets you require.

## Do I Qualify?

Certain benefits are "means-tested". This means that you are only entitled to them if you are unemployed or your income falls below certain fixed levels. Some have an age qualification. Other benefits come as an automatic right. A few, like sickness benefit (which can apply to the unemployed too) depend on the amount of National Insurance contributions you may have paid in the past. However do not be put off claiming a benefit just because you may be unsure of whether you are entitled to it or because you already receive some other benefit. Make a claim anyway. The DHSS will soon tell you if you are excluded. Being self-employed is rarely any problem. If you have any difficulty completing or understanding a form and you cannot find a helpful DHSS officer, seek the aid of a friend or your local Citizens Advice Bureau. If you are not satisfied that your local DHSS are correct in what they tell you, dial 100 and ask for Freefone DHSS for an independent regional office view.

## Other Sources Of Benefits

Your local council will probably be responsible for rent/rate rebates (even on owner-occupier or private tenant accommodation). They can probably help if you are an invalid or look after someone who is. Many councils operate countless other benefits too, especially for your children. Again, you need to obtain their most recent comprehensive guide and follow up by getting detailed literature as necessary.

Your tax office deals with your tax allowances. If your tax is dealt with miles away, a local office will usually liaise for you. These allowances make part of your income, tax free. You need to make sure the tax people are fully aware of your age, marital and family status, whether you have a dependent relative, or disablement in the family, or have lost your spouse and so forth. Once more, scrutinise information fact sheets which they will freely send to you. If you pay tax and your income suddenly falls start the process of claiming a tax refund at once.

The Education Authority responsible for your area will have a welfare office and a bewildering array of benefits which your family may enjoy while children are at school (even after age 16) or if they have become students. Ferret hard to discover what is what and stake your claims with whichever departments organise each item.

Apart from these sources remember: a second-rate employer may need to be chased over redundancy payments or in connection with injury at work; for unusual problems do not overlook the possibility that there may be a charity able to offer all sorts of free help; legal aid may be appropriate via solicitors operating the scheme. All such potential sources of help can be researched via your Citizens Advice Bureau.

If you are up to your neck in debt you really must claim every allowable benefit from the right place at the right time (some are lost or reduced if you are not quick off the mark, e.g. unemployment pay). So take a rigorous look at all the areas in which you might be entitled to benefits. No one else will do it so well for you.

Criteria for establishing whether you are entitled to most benefits are strictly governed by law, and there are well established appeals procedures to deal with complaints. If you feel you ought to be entitled to a particular benefit but your claim has been turned down, appeal in writing against the decision.

You will usually be allowed to present your case before a local tribunal who deal with such matters. Or you might be able to take things to Court on legal aid. If you think you would have difficulty presenting your case you can have a friend or some other person take charge of this for you. Even if there is a hearing it will not always be necessary for you to attend in person. If you are clear in your own mind that you are entitled to a benefit you are claiming do not be put off from making an appeal because of a fear of officialdom. Misuse of official power is just what such appeal procedures are there to prevent.

## Redundancy Payments

Most full-time employees who are made redundant are entitled to compensation. If you are made redundant, act quickly to secure your rights. Lodge a written claim immediately with your ex-employer. Do not delay or you may lose out. Appeal to an Industrial Tribunal if your ex-employer does not pay up within a few months.

If the firm you work for goes bankrupt or into liquidation you are still entitled to any redundancy payments for which you qualify. In this case make a claim at your local office of the Department of Employment. They take over responsibility for such a payment where there is no money available from the business.

# 9

# UNEMPLOYMENT

Unemployment invariably brings in its wake a wide range of financial problems. The unemployed have also got to contend with a number of psychological and practical hurdles. Anyone who has been unemployed for any length of time will understand how life quickly becomes dominated and restrained by tight finances.

Feelings of depression can rapidly set in and a loss of morale may be experienced. These feelings need to be countered with a positive set of attitudes to deal with the difficulties you will have to face.

If you are married with a family, hold a "family conference" to discuss how you are going to cope as a family. Unless your children are very young they should be included in this conference. Children often have more understanding of life than adults sometimes give them credit for. They will certainly be able to appreciate the stark financial straitjacket that faces the family until you land a new job.

A stringent financial strategy will have to assume top priority. Some harsh decisions may need to be taken very quickly, such as giving up a rented television and video recorder.

A careful examination of the family budget must be carried out to see where savings can be made. If you have been unemployed for a while and "let things go" in the hope that a new job will turn up, it is doubly important that you pull your reins in now.

There is an understandable tendency amongst some unemployed people to bury their heads in the sand like an ostrich and fail to take such steps. Make sure that you do not fall into this trap. If you are in it – then pull yourself out of that category, now. Make a fresh start. Get your finances into survival shape *before* you need to. Failing to face up to difficult financial decisions quickly leads to disaster.

One advantage that an unemployed person has over an employed one is time. This time should be turned to maximum advantage. A detailed survey should be made of all the financial aspects of your life. Letters should be sent off to creditors if necessary (see Chapter 7) informing them of your unemployment. It may be worth a visit to some of them.

If you are buying your home go to see your building society manager immediately to discuss how you might deal with your mortgage repayments. Even if you do not owe money to the bank it is a good plan to see the manager straightaway. Otherwise you may sow a needless doubt in his mind about your ability to keep frank with him. If you can, arrange an overdraft facility ready for when you may need it. Or it may be a case of trying to reschedule existing borrowings. Use your time wisely and well to keep on top of your financial difficulties.

Think up ways to reduce your household expenditure. It is surprising how much can be cut back.

Sort out your benefits' position straightaway as outlined in the previous Chapter. Study the rules and regulations which specifically affect unemployment pay so that you cannot unwittingly lose out.

## Who Cannot Have Unemployment Pay?
Self-employed people cannot claim unemployment benefit as such. However, they are entitled to certain other benefits if they have insufficient money coming in to make ends meet. Self-employed people often miss out on claiming benefits they are entitled to because they pride themselves on their self-sufficiency. Swallow your pride if you are self-employed and in financial trouble, and check with the DHSS or a Citizens Advice Bureau to see what benefits you can claim. You can be refused benefit if you place "unreasonable

restrictions" on the sort of work, pay and conditions which you are prepared to accept if you are offered a job. However, you can insist that your physical condition be taken into account if you refuse to accept a job offer (usually this will be on medical advice). You can also demand that due account is made of your normal occupation and the time that has elapsed since you became unemployed.

Up to six weeks' benefit can be withheld if:

1   You have just been sacked for "misconduct". This does not necessarily mean that moral blame was attached to your conduct, rather that your behaviour was such as to make you unfit to do the job. Examples of this are disobedience, faulty workmanship or idleness.
2   You left your last job voluntarily and without good reason.
3   You do not attend an interview arranged for you, or you attend the interview but do not try to get the job.

Part-time working while unemployed reduces unemployment pay entitlement. You normally lose one-sixth of your weekly unemployment pay for every day you work. You must declare if you have worked. Very strict fines and prison sentences have been given to people who "moonlight", i.e. do other jobs whilst continuing to claim full unemployment pay.

Pensions: If you are receiving an early pension of some sort, you will not be entitled to full unemployment benefit.

If unemployment pay is denied you, there will be other means-tested benefits which can be claimed. What you get will depend on your overall financial circumstances.

**Further Help For The Unemployed**
There is a wide range of financial and other help that may be valuable to an unemployed person. For example, at the time of writing there are re-training allowances, job search and employment transfer benefits, and employment rehabilitation allowances. Find out what these offer and check your

eligibility at your Job Centre or Employment Office.

## Positive Steps To Be Taken

There is only one way to deal with unemployment and that is to treat it as a "job". If you are unemployed you now have the full-time occupation of dealing with your finances and job-hunting. With the application of some vitality, overcoming both these difficulties can be turned into what amounts to a trail-blazing contest, with you as the winner all the way. If you have a family involve them in this "game" as well.

It all helps to avoid the "unemployment blues". Most people have inside them a stock of untapped and undreamed-of abilities. We humans are very adaptable and that includes you. Being out of work can be a time to take stock. You may decide you need further education or some skill training before going for a job (if you can afford to survive meanwhile) or you may decide to aim at both – a job to bring in some money while you tackle a qualification which will lead to better prospects. (Some employers will allow time off for studies or training, so you could enquire.)

## Education

Forget about failure at school, or lamenting success there which seems to have deserted you since. Many people are "late developers" and only reach their full mental skills and abilities long after leaving school. Life is a school and if you decide to return to education you are likely to be surprised to discover what a head-start you will have over younger people.

Most adults who return to education do extremely well. They tend to work harder than youngsters and achieve better results in examinations. It does not matter if you do not have a single CSE or "O" level (or GCSE) to your name. Aim straight for the top.

There are many ways in which you can return to education. Your best starting point is to find out where the local Adult Education Centre is. Every local education authority runs courses for adults. All of these centres have counsellors who can advise. Major libraries carry a wealth of reference books you can scan through, both to discover things you might not have thought of, and to help you make up your mind about which qualification(s) you want to head for.

If you are of a brave and adventurous spirit you can embark directly on a degree course through the Open University. There are fees to be paid but reductions are often made for the unemployed. This was the course of action that the author of this book took at a difficult time in life. Ultimately it led to the writing of this book.

You may feel you lack the confidence to advance your education in this way. Excellent preparatory courses are available throughout the country that enable adults to enter directly into higher education later. Seek the nearest.

The sky is the limit so do not let gloom-merchants dissuade you. If you always wanted to be a teacher, a solicitor or an accountant there is nothing to stop you unless you lack determination.

One word of warning I must give; if you decide to embark on a career in higher education, make sure that you check realistically on potential career opportunities connected with the course you intend to take. There are many thousands of ex-bus drivers, failed or retired sportsmen etc., who have obtained good class exam passes only to find their career dreams frustrated because their qualifications have little practical application. This applies particularly to qualifications in arts subjects. So make sure you think far into the future. Look for abilities that will not easily be swamped by man's inventive genius and ones that do not lead only to those jobs which are always the first to be cut back. Note that government jobs, local or central, having been the most consistent "growth industry" since the war, are overdue for massive job losses when world economic reality finally bites.

**Training Courses**

There is a huge variety of training courses available from colleges of further education and other institutions. You can learn hairdressing, carpentry, catering, etc.

So if you are unskilled but daunted by the thought of higher education there are still countless opportunities to acquire a practical skill that will give you personal satisfaction and help you find work. Enquire at the place concerned, via the Local Education Authority, or at Job Centres, about the kind of courses on offer and any grants or training allowances that go with them. For something very specialised there may be a course outside your area which you can get help to attend.

**Job Seeking**

Your finances may be such that it is imperative that you find a job as soon as possible. The author of this book was a careers teacher for some years and was struck by the ineptitude that many young people showed in trying to find jobs. So many adults show little more sense than these youngsters, I make no apology for setting out some basic rules to think about:

1 If you do not apply for a job you will not get one. (An employer will not come looking for you unless you are extremely lucky.) Look for jobs reasonably within your abilities and *apply*. If nothing else, you will begin to sharpen up your interview technique and learn about which jobs you *do not* want.

2 Written job applications need to be neat and accompanied by a typed note listing your work achievements to date, personal details such as age, marital status etc., and brief details of your education. One side of a page is enough! So do not wax lyrical about irrelevant long-past detail.

3 Arrive for interviews on time and well-presented. Make sure you are clean, especially your shoes. Shoes *are* noticed.

4  Looking for a job is a full-time task. Make sure you
   spend most of your effort on it. Act, every day.

In the experience of the author the people who find jobs
are the ones that follow these rules.

Out of a hundred possible employers it does not matter if
ninety-nine say no, so long as one says yes. You only need
one job. The author of this book, whilst searching for his
first teaching job, made over three hundred hand-written
applications to obtain four job interviews. The outcome was
that he clinched a suitable post. Never give up. There is
always a job somewhere for the person who is continually
trying. Make sure that you are that person.


**An "Inside" Job**
Lots of the best jobs go to people already in the
organisations concerned – known quantities – safe to
promote. Thus there is much to be said for getting in
*somewhere*, even at the bottom, regardless of pride or
whether you once had some far superior job. From there you
can demonstrate your guts for hard, intelligent work. You
can indicate your willingness to learn about what other
people at the concern do, and to step-in and help wherever
anyone is under pressure. You are well placed to put yourself
up for it when the right position comes free. Good
management will not often let good workers slip through
their fingers; they notice and offer promotion before you
ask. Remember, the good boss who did not himself once
sweep the floor has not been born. If it turns out to be a bad
outfit you are still bound to have learned something, and
being in a job is always useful backing for your next move. If
the field the job was in proves to be not for you, that
discovery helps you choose another occupation with more
chance you will like it.


**The Real "Blues"**
I spoke earlier of countering the "blues". Sometimes

reaction to unemployment – perhaps worsened by other misfortunes – brings on depression to the point where a person is ill with it. Too many of our hard-pressed GPs in the National Health Service are no-hopers where it comes to understanding or dealing with this condition. The system does not allow them time to deal adequately with its accurate diagnosis, never mind the time to support the patient with guidance about how to cope with the all-pervading negative thoughts which are its most debilitating feature. Can you blame the doctors for not wanting to sacrifice dispro-portionate surgery time on this illness when the care they give other patients would have to suffer? The common-place routine which results is a prescription for catch-all pills doled out with a few words of uselessly paternalistic advice, with the main object of curtailing the patient's visit to the minimum time.

To be fair some doctors are this quick, and they do get it right; but this fact will not be much use to you if your "blues" still persist to the degree that they dampen your spirits, sap your concentration and prevent you going after a new job efficiently and effectively. If that happens for more than about a month with hardly any brighter moments, you may need considerably more attention and skill.

The chances are such depression stems mainly from the way you think about the trouble you are in. The right pills can restore your energy, a bit like a tonic, and may be vital to get you restarted, but there is a very good way to help yourself too. Confide how you feel (write down some of those fleeting negative thoughts ready) to one or two who have gone through unemployment in a psychologically strong style and who have succeeded in getting back into work recently. Compare your attitudes with theirs, and build, from what you learn, a cocoon of positive good-thinking to carry you through. You will find people are flattered and pleased to help. Just sharing the burden of your difficult feelings lifts your spirits, never mind the game plan for being positive which this action will place in your grasp.

Occasionally depression arises more in the body than in the mind. This sort can come on even when no pressing problems like unemployment are afoot. It is a different "animal" rather more outside conscious control (in the same way as migraine might be); it needs medical intervention at specialist level.

In the event of any long lasting depressive episode you must go back to your doctor and insist on proper time, or referral. It often needs considerable care and time in diagnosis to identify how much the causes may be reactions to events and to what extent they may be bodily sourced, before appropriate medical treatment can be chosen.

Whether such an illness is of the first type or the second, or combined in some degree, rest assured your confidence and vitality can be restored. You can hasten the day with the game plan I have suggested. *You* can seek out the right doctor for the medical side of things. Remember that, like bank managers (see page 52), if you cannot get on with one, you need another; so do not hesitate to change till you find one who talks sense.

You may be depressed but *you* have still got brains and judgment. If you conclude that your present doctor is no help on this illness there is one to be found somewhere nearby who is the opposite, a genius. Rest not till you find him or her. There is no need to waste time with a doctor you neither trust nor believe has the necessary skill and experience. Politely but firmly demand to see the best in the business. You will know at once when you have found the person for you. Enlist the help of a relative, a clergyman or similar respected individual if you meet trouble over being referred or have difficulty persuading someone to see you. Your local Community Health Council (see 'phone book) may be able to help you in this connection.

# 10

# COURT ORDERS AND ADMINISTRATION ORDERS

**County Court Orders**
Most people get very upset when they receive a summons from a County Court. They are often confused as to how to deal with it.

**Types Of Summons**
Apart from a bankruptcy petition (which I come to in Part Two) there are two types of summons. One is known as a fixed date summons and the other is called a default summons. The first is issued when a claim is being made other than for a sum of money, e.g. for the repossession of your home or the recovery of goods. The second would be for a claim purely over money.

A fixed date summons fixes a date, normally about six weeks ahead, on which both parties to the summons must attend. It may be a preliminary hearing, sometimes called a "pre-trial review". The date of this hearing will be shown on your summons and you must either attend yourself or send someone else to represent you. If the date clashes with some other important engagement, you can ask the Court to alter it as long as you ask promptly. Apply late and it can involve you in extra expense.

The registrar can decide not to have a pre-trial review, and may instead proceed directly to the main hearing. Practice varies from Court to Court. Make sure you understand the status of the hearing to which you are being called.

In a default summons the parties are not in the first

instance called to attend Court. The summons is simply to force you to pay up at once. If you do not pay, or do not deliver an admission (see below) with an offer of payment, or a defence or counterclaim within fourteen days after service of the summons upon you, then a judgment may well be entered against you. You will be ordered to pay your creditor immediately and, unless you do, he may then be in a position to make you bankrupt very fast.

## Summons' Documents

When a Court serves a summons on you a form for admission, or for defence and counterclaim, is enclosed with it. Using this form correctly is vital to inform the Court of your circumstances and/or to prevent any instant-pay-up order such as just described. Get help from your Citizens Advice Bureau or a friend if necessary.

## Defence Or Counterclaim

If you do not admit that you owe the money, or believe you owe less, complete the defence section and return the form to the Court within fourteen days. Your creditor will be sent a copy by the Court who will then arrange a preliminary hearing, or fix a date for arbitration or for a trial.

## Admission

If you admit the claim but you want time to pay, you must answer the questions on the form as to your means and liabilities and set out any offer you wish to put forward. Again you should return this form to the Court quickly. They will send a copy to your creditor. It is up to your creditor to decide whether or not to accept your offer and let the Court know.

If he does accept, the Court will formalise the arrangement by writing to both of you. Failure to stick to your agreement at any stage will mean your creditor can take further drastic steps against you at once.

If your creditor will not agree to what you suggest you can pay, the Court will fix an appointment when the judge/registrar can decide how quickly the debt is to be paid. Both you and your creditor will be notified and should attend the Court. If you are unable to go you can write to the Court asking for another date, or (though I would not recommend this) you can ask the Court to deal with the matter in your absence.

Appointments of this kind are called "disposals", and are quite informal. You have no need to be frightened about attending. If your creditor comes he is entitled to ask you about your means, so if you have any documentary evidence as to your earnings or property, take it with you. The registrar can also question you about the answers you have given on your form. When he has listened to both you and your creditor, he will decide by what size of instalments you will have to pay. It is unlikely that he will ask you to pay faster than you can reasonably afford. Most creditors will accept the decision of the registrar about how much you should pay; therefore, so long as you keep up the ordered payments, you are likely to be safe from further action. However, if the debt is sufficiently large, your creditor may be in a position to press for your bankruptcy even though the cost of this is heavy and will have to be borne by him.

## The Purpose Of A Pre-Trial Review

A pre-trial review usually takes place informally in private. You will be asked to sit down and you need not expect a judge complete with wig. The review is really no more than a discussion between the registrar and the two parties to decide how the action is to be dealt with. If you do not attend this review your creditor may be able to obtain judgment against you in your absence, after proving his case.

Go.

You may have to give evidence. The registrar will ask you to stand to take the oath but you can usually sit after that. Remember to take any bills, receipts, letters or documents that could help. The registrar will look at any papers and ask

you and/or your creditor to explain matters more fully to
him where he so wishes. You are entitled to ask for further
information from your creditor and he or she has a similar
right of you.

Having established the facts the registrar will try to see if
the matter can be resolved without proceeding to trial. Often
he is able, after discussion, to reach an agreement between
the two parties. However if dispute remains or there are
special reasons he may suggest arbitration or refer the matter
for a full hearing.

**Arbitration**
Disputes over fairly small sums are very often referred to
arbitration. Disputes over large sums may also be dealt with
this way. Arbitration procedures are less formal than a full
trial and the costs for both parties are thereby kept down.

Both sides usually agree in advance to be bound by
whatever ruling results from the arbitration. You are entitled
to see beforehand any documents that your creditor intends
to use and vice versa. The registrar may suggest the sort of
evidence you should bring to the hearing and whether an
expert witness should attend. However, he will be guarded in
his advice because he must not be seen to be favouring either
party.

If arbitration is not agreed upon then a date will be set for
a trial. This will be a very formal affair and you will have to
give evidence on oath standing in the witness box. You must
avoid saying what someone else told you otherwise the judge
or registrar will stop you because this is known as "hearsay"
and is not allowed. On the other hand, you can repeat what
your opponent or witnesses have said because they can be
asked about it when they give evidence. Each side can cross-
examine the other. Afterwards the judge or registrar will ask
questions to clarify problem areas and will probably make a
decision then and there.

If the case is a difficult one the Court may reserve
judgment and appoint a further date for you to attend Court
when judgment will be given.

**General Points**

Millions of cases go through the County Courts each year and in many of them debtors do not bother to turn up at Court or even reply to the Court papers. This is very foolish. It leaves you wide open to a harsh judgment in favour of your creditor.

In Court it is better to have an adviser. If you do not know anyone suitable ask your local Citizens Advice Bureau who may know someone, or may even have a specialist of their own in advising and representing debtors in Court. You do not necessarily need a solicitor, although you may be able to obtain one on legal aid.

**What If I Cannot Afford To Pay What I Have Been Ordered To Pay?**

You can apply for a variation order. Visit or send a letter to the Court where your case was heard applying for a new order at a rate you can manage. (See page 98). You have nothing to lose by making such an application, everything to gain.

**Can Money Be Taken From My Wages?**

If payments set by a Court at an earlier date are not being kept up, your creditor can approach the Court and ask them to make an attachment of earnings order. This orders *your employer* to deduct money from your wages and pay it directly to the Court. Should one be proposed in your case make sure you complete and return any Court documents sent to you. You can be sent to prison for contempt of Court if you fail. The Court has the power to decide against such a step. So it is vital to explain to the Court if this would cause you great embarrassment for example in a small office, or if it might lead to the loss of your job. These orders can also be disputed later, for example if your circumstances change, by applying back to the Court.

**Administration Orders**

An administration order is a sort of small man's bankruptcy. It is useful when you have a lot of debts. However, the total must fall below a level that is reviewed from time to time. Check with your Citizens Advice Bureau or County Court office for the present rule. A mortgage may or may not have to count within this total depending on your general financial circumstances. If you are self-employed refer to the next chapter; your problems are likely to fall outside the scope of such an order anyway.

An administration order enables you to have the assistance and supervision of the Court to sort out and organise all your debts whilst being protected from harassment by many different creditors each using different methods to obtain their money. It means effectively you obtain an honourable discharge short of bankruptcy. Out of your earnings you have to pay a single monthly amount to the Court, which then distributes the money to your creditors in a fair and just way. One bonus of the system is that all your creditors benefit rather than the most forceful ones bankrupting you to start with.

Most debtors are unaware that it is up to them to take the initiative and ask the Court to help by organising an administration order. As a result administration orders are not used very frequently. Many solicitors and Court officials lack expertise in handling them anyway and some County Courts are simply reluctant to make such orders because of the amount of work involved. However, although the Courts cannot get involved like this unless at least one judgment debt has been made against you, for the most part they are helpful in advising debtors about possible solutions.

The main effect of such an order is that your creditors will find it very difficult thereafter to enforce their individual debts except by agreement of the Court. Understandably a landlord still may have a strong case to claim for up to six months' rent and you should be aware that any creditor may yet present a bankruptcy petition with the agreement of the Court, or ask for the matter to be referred to a higher Court if not satisfied. However, in my experience most creditors leave these matters to the Court and in practice accept whatever dividend they are paid.

An attachment of earnings order is sometimes used in conjunction with an administration order, especially if you are in a steady job. This may be a blessing because if you fail to make the payments to the Court they can decide to end the administration order immediately and put you into bankruptcy. So make sure you maintain your payments.

## Common Legal Queries

Suppose you have already paid the debt owed to one of your creditors when you receive a summons from him. Who pays the Court costs? So long as the creditor was justified in taking the proceedings and gave you ample warning the Court will normally order you to pay. You are only likely to persuade the registrar not to make an order for costs against you, if, for example, you can show with a dated receipt or recorded delivery ticket that your creditor must have received the money from you before the summons was issued.

## Setting Aside A Judgment Or Award

A debt summons does not have to be handed to you personally so it is possible you may not even know you have been sued. Even when you have received the summons, you may not have been able to do anything about it within the time allowed. Either way (though you would need a good excuse in the latter case), you may not know that a judgment has already been made against you until you receive a copy of the Court order through the post, or when a bailiff calls at your home to seize goods in satisfaction of your debt.

If you find yourself in this position you should go without delay to the Court offices where the officials should be able to tell you about the claim. Take the Court order with you, or if you have only heard about the case from the bailiff ask him for the case number so that the officials can trace the necessary papers.

A judgment that has been entered when no defence was filed or because you did not attend the Court can still be set aside by a registrar. This will depend upon all of the circumstances. For example if the summons was not properly served and you had no knowledge of the proceedings, you are entitled to have the judgment set aside as a matter of right. If you have failed to file a defence but can still convince the registrar there are good grounds for setting aside the judgment he may do so. It is not necessarily in your own interest to try because costs would definitely be loaded against you in the absence of any real defence. He may also require you to pay costs that your creditor has incurred so far as a result of your default, and he may decide to order you to pay some or all of the money your creditor is claiming into the Court as well, to remain there until after the action has been tried.

### How To Make An Application To A Court
A simple letter asking for what you want is all that is required. Alternatively find out from the Court if there is an appropriate form specially available for the purpose you require. Always make sure you include the case details and number (from the Court order or summons), relevant dates, your own full address and that of whoever has taken you to Court. You could lay it out like this:-


Date                          In the................County Court
                              Case No. & date.....................
              Between ........................................................
              And ....................................................(Self)

### NOTICE OF APPLICATION
Dear Sir,
    As defendant in the above proceedings I wish to apply for (STATE THE NATURE AND GROUNDS OF THE APPLICATION)
    ... I look forward to your decision.

Yours faithfully,

....................

If there is a special form but it is complicated, a Court official can help you fill it in or explain legal terminology. You can deliver your letter/form to the Court yourself or post it in (best to use recorded delivery or registered post). *Keep a copy.*

The reasons you might give, for example when asking for a judgment to be set aside, could be along the lines such as one of these perhaps with a little more detail:

1) I did not receive the summons.
2) I was away from home and did not receive the summons in time to put forward my defence.
3) I was ill in hospital at the time of the hearing and was unable to attend.
4) I have only recently uncovered the documents necessary for my defence.

Two extra copies of your application are required, one for your creditor, the other for the registrar. The Court will inform you of the date and time when the application will be heard.

## Service Of The Applicaiton

*Such an application also has to be served (delivered to) your creditor.* Some Courts may send the application to your creditor; others expect you to do this yourself. Find out who is to do it because when your application is heard, the registrar will have to satisfy himself that your creditor has been given sufficient notice. If you have to serve the notice yourself, either hand it to your creditor personally or post it by recorded delivery so that you can produce the receipt slip to the registrar as evidence that you have delivered it. It must reach your creditor at least two days before the application is heard.

### Attending The Application

It is important to go or to arrange for someone else to attend on your behalf; otherwise your application is most likely to be refused. Although the registrar can deal with the application in your absence you should regard this as a last resort. If neither you nor anyone in your place can go then at the very least write to the registrar explaining why, and, if it was your responsibility to serve your application on your creditor, confirm how and when you did so. Enclose the postal receipt if appropriate.

### Solicitors

Little mention has been made of solicitors. This has been deliberate because the average person can deal adequately with Court procedures in a County Court under his or her own steam, possibly assisted by a friend or someone from a Citizens Advice Bureau. You do not really need a solicitor to deal with most legal actions over debt. However, if you are unduly nervous in such situations, or your defence is extremely complicated, or the amounts involved are very large, I must advise you to seek professional help. You may have to pay for it but your local Citizens Advice Bureau can advise you if you are entitled to legal aid and may be able to suggest a specialist solicitor.

### Further Actions

A creditor dissatisfied with a County Court decision may refer the matter to a higher Court for review, hoping for a better result from his point of view. This may lead you to the High Court. Occasionally a High Court writ is the first step against you anyway.

### High Court Writs

A writ from a High Court is extremely serious because normally only large debts involving several thousand pounds are dealt with there. Often, the service of such a writ is a preliminary to a bankruptcy petition. If you dispute the debt you will be well advised to seek the advice of a solicitor immediately. Unlike a County Court a High Court has no facilities to accept payment by instalments or to organise an administration order, or any of the other helpful possibilities already discussed. If it makes an order against you bailiffs act at once. Failing sale of your goods raising enough to cover your debts, your bankruptcy will be imminent. (See page 49.) Therefore, while all Court orders should be taken very seriously, a High Court writ means a dire threat is being made against you. Immediate expert advice and action is your best hope if you wish to avoid or at least lessen the unhappy consequences. It may be a case for petitioning your own bankruptcy. Read Part Two of this book carefully to help you decide.

# 11

# BUSINESS DEBTS

Self-employed people running their own business very often
run into debt. A large percentage of all bankruptcies involve
them. Not only does the self-employed businessman tend to
have many more creditors than an individual, any of whom
might be prepared to force a bankruptcy, the Inland
Revenue and the Customs and Excise seem quicker to hound
businessmen down the avenue of bankruptcy nowadays,
knowing they will thereby secure the preferential payment
they then enjoy from any assets.

Take the case of Tom Johnson who runs a small building
repair business. He has been trading successfully for four
years but badly underestimated on a recent contract, losing
several thousand pounds. He is now midway into a
profitable contract and has built in safeguards which make
repetition of the earlier disaster improbable, but he is under
pressure from several creditors. Tom has the following
debts:

| | | | |
|---|---|---|---|
| Creditor A: | £1,500.00 | Creditor F: | £25.00 |
| Creditor B: | £800.00 | Creditor G: | £1,160.00 |
| Creditor C: | £250.00 | Creditor H: | £300.00 |
| Creditor D: | £1,400.00 | Creditor I: | £2,400.00 |
| Creditor E: | £80.00 | Bank Overdraft: | £8,251.00 |
| | | Total Debts: | £16,166.00 |

Besides his home which is mortgaged Tom's major assets
are some leftover building materials, his van and his tools
and equipment. He could sell these but then he could no
longer carry on his business which he is confident will
prosper in the future. Tom has no means of predicting what

his future income will be with certainty, so he cannot make offers of regular monthly payments to his creditors in the way suggested in Chapter 7.

## A Moratorium

The best tactic for Tom is to appoint a solicitor or an accountant who will take professional charge of his affairs temporarily, and try to arrange some form of moratorium. This is an arrangement under which the creditors, or at least the major ones, agree to a delay in the payment of their debts and that they will not take legal action in the meantime. It has to depend on goodwill because at no stage do they give up their right to sue for the balance of what they are owed.

Tom's appointed advisor should write to the creditors concerned setting out his proposals and explaining why the difficulties arose. In his letter he will offer, subject to their agreement, to take charge of all monies Tom receives. His prospective commitment will be to manage Tom's finances so that all his debts are cleared as fast as income allows. He may seek permission to clear tiny creditors (who could cause more trouble than they are worth and take undue administrative time) early, so that the number of people involved is minimised. He may also have to ask that Tom be allowed a "subsistence" income. Otherwise, the undertaking will be to make proportionate stage payments to every main creditor as often as possible till the plan is fulfilled. He will mention that if creditors prefer to appoint someone of their own choosing to administer such a plan they are free to do so and he will invite any questions or suggestions. Without committing himself or Tom to a rigid timetable he will probably indicate a hoped-for timescale to complete the operation. Finally he will ask them to let him know as soon as possible if they are agreeable to his putting the arrangement in hand. A note from Tom should accompany this letter confirming that he will be bound by the proposed scheme and expressing his sincere hope that the way forward suggested will receive acceptance by all concerned.

Because the proposals are presented by a professional

third party, Tom's creditors can see that he is serious in his intentions and that they will all be treated fairly. It is reasonable for them to agree to sensible proposals of this kind.

The bank may be helpful in co-ordinating a moratorium approach of this sort. Depending how many creditors there are and how well he knows them, Tom may choose to deliver his advisor's letter personally, so that he can explain the position and get the friendlier ones on his side first, in the hope that tougher ones may thereby be persuaded to join what, after all, is an act of faith in himself.

The Inland Revenue and/or the Customs and Excise can exhibit varying degrees of accommodation about a moratorium in respect of taxes, and are generally less willing to go along than trade creditors usually are. You may have to reach some understanding with them at the outset so that the other creditors can be informed of any potential difficulty taxwise. (They will no doubt be aware of the notorious preferential status enjoyed by the taxman.)

Tom will have to pay a fee for all his advisor's work but it should not be large and will be a small price to pay to avert bankruptcy.

I must stress that to admit to your creditors that you are unable to meet all liabilities on time is to commit an act of bankruptcy, which a creditor could try to use as the basis of a bankruptcy petition. So the moratorium route out of trouble is not without some risk. Other times when it might be a worthwhile approach to business debts that have temporarily grown topsy are, for example, when you have a lot of money owed to you from one of your customers not due for payment soon enough, or maybe overdue and already involving you in enforcement action. Perhaps you have substantial orders held up till supplies of some material jammed in a dock strike come through.

In moratoriums where a lot of assets influence their agreement to help over a cash-flow problem, creditors are understandably concerned to make sure that those assets are not wasted. You must expect that they may want to set up an informal committee of inspection with permission to supervise the professional advisor you have asked to deal with your affairs. That should not be any problem but you may find difficulty in obtaining further credit from your suppliers so that you can continue to trade generally. It is therefore wise to discuss at the outset arrangements which will allow you to trade at least at a level where you can earn sufficient profit to carry out your proposals.

## Informal Arrangements To Settle Debts For Less

By this it is meant that you try to persuade all of your creditors to accept smaller sums in full settlement than you actually owe. Informal Arrangements work best when there are only one or two creditors. It is very unlikely that a large body of creditors will ALL agree. There is always one who will petition for bankruptcy and negate your hopes of avoiding it. It is likely to mean the end of your business because no creditor will want to risk the same position twice but at least you may steer clear of official bankruptcy.

One aspect of creditors making you bankrupt is that it can make it easier for them to write off the debt, and reclaim any VAT they have paid on your debts. On the other hand they will be aware of the huge costs of taking you to Court or petitioning for bankruptcy. They will take account of such factors before deciding to accept a reduced settlement from you. Unless you can still find enough money to offer all creditors proportionate sums that make commercial sense for them to accept, you will not stand much chance of success. Approaching all creditors like this would be an act of bankruptcy because you are admitting you cannot pay all your debts. Any one of them can force a bankruptcy as a result. However, if your position is very serious you may have no option but to take this chance.

Note that settlement sums agreed are not necessarily binding on your creditors, unless the Informal Arrangement is formalised under seal. So you should make sure that the paperwork is organised through a solicitor who understands the proper procedure.

If a third party pays a reduced settlement in return for your being released from your debt this is much more likely

to be legally binding. However, you should both be wary.
Law and its interpretation in Court frequently seem unfair
and often beyond understanding. Recently a man steppéd
in and paid his friend's debt just in time to obtain the
adjournment of a bankruptcy petition. Unfortunately the
debtor was eventually adjudicated bankrupt on the petition
of another firm owed money. The creditor who had been
paid was made to give back the money he had received, not
to the friend but to the debtor's trustee in bankruptcy. Not
only did his friend lose his money, the debtor went bankrupt
anyway. The Court took the view that it could not reverse
the fact of the gift (a personal decision anyway) but that it
did have jurisdiction over the disposition of all the assets of
the debtor – including, mindful of its timing, the gift money.

### Limited Companies – A Common Misunderstanding
Do not imagine you can seek protection by becoming a
limited company, once you are in debt. A limited company is
a separate legal entity. You have to think of it as a separate
person from yourself.

Take the fictional example of Sarah Sweeney who has
been building up a fish farm. She has debts of £20,000 in her
own name and has only just turned the corner into profit,
though not yet enough to cover all the interest. At this point
Sarah sets up a company called Sarah Sweeney Limited. She
informs all her creditors and they agree to extend credit to
the new company.

Sarah makes the error of assuming that the debts she
incurred in her own name will now be the responsibility of
the limited company. Though she is confident the business
will soon be earning good profits, Sarah feels happier that if
unforeseeable disaster strikes, her personal assets will
remain safe.

Suppose that, within a month, two competitors start up,
there is a fierce local price war and, under such pressure
Sarah's fish farm business collapses. To show why her
thinking was wrong let's examine the debt position at the
point the business folds. Of the debts invoiced to *her* name

before the company was formed, we'll assume £5,000 have been paid off. Meanwhile however, £10,000 of debt has accumulated, invoiced to the limited company since that time.

In simple terms, if when the company assets are sold only £5,000 is raised, those suppliers owed the £10,000 will only get half their money. The limited liability protects Sarah from any further demands there. The bad news is that Sarah is still responsible for the £15,000 that remains outstanding in her own name. Her creditors will almost certainly put her into personal bankruptcy to get what they can.

If you are in business in your own name and would prefer the protection of a limited company you need to be extremely careful about how you handle the transition if there are going to be substantial debts existing at the changeover date. Especially beware of simply arranging for the company to take over existing acounts held in your own name; in law you could find you end up in Sarah's predicament if insolvency was ever to hit you.

It is worth mentioning here that one new proposal of revised insolvency law currently in preparation may be to bar directors involved in a company which becomes insolvent from holding any directorship thereafter, for several years. The only exception might be if such a director proved to the satisfaction of a Court that he or she had taken all possible steps to minimise potential losses for creditors. If you are involved in any directorships you may need to check if this is now law and in just what form. The sort of proof that a Court might accept, though there would be no guarantee, could be minutes of meetings held during the period prior to the insolvency which clearly recorded a particular director's dissent on matters of policy later shown to be the cause of the company failure.

## Personal Guarantees

Increasingly banks and sometimes trade creditors ask directors of limited liability companies to give various personal financial guarantees. Directors sign these without enough thought, perhaps to gain improved loan terms, maybe because times are bad, or to enable them to borrow more and expand their company faster. With 20/20 hindsight it is invariably easy to see that undue optimism or blinkers were at work at the time.

Sometimes a guarantee is limited to a fixed amount of money but people forget that such a guarantee might be called in just when they are hard-pressed on their own finances too, and that the combination could lead to bankruptcy. Perhaps more commonly a guarantee will take the form of the full collateral of your home or some other major asset. If the company fails you have to pay up the amount stated in the guarantee. Usually the home (or the asset) has to go, so as to hand over the proceeds to the holder of the guarantee. Although on a stipulated size of guarantee such as this you will not then be held responsible for the balance of any other debts that the limited company may have, the trauma can be awful. The complications which can emerge over the house if you also get involved in divorce (when half its value may be subject to claim by your spouse) can pitch you into a further layer of troubles which will make the first lot look like a side-show.

If you are unfortunate enough to have signed an unlimited personal guarantee your company may as well not have been limited. You stand to be cleaned out. Obviously it may be a problem not to alarm the lender but you must move as fast as possible towards gaining some limitation on such a guarantee, on your way to reaching a less draconian form of security to satisfy your lender. Personal guarantees are very nasty. The growth in their use stems in the U.K. from the effective lack of competitive banking available, letting bully-boy bankers cover their backsides against any real risk sharing, all the way from the bank . . .

You should be aware that death is not final in regard to a personal guarantee. The guarantee can flow past your death, leaving your estate potentially liable. Keep a copy of any such guarantee alongside your Will so that your executors will know immediately that it exists. They will have the problem of being unable to distribute from your estate until they have been able to negotiate with the lender to release the estate from the guarantee. If the business was extremely dependent on your being alive and working this release could prove almost impossible to negotiate. Think through before you sign.

When a lender takes a guarantee of collateral against a family home (as for example might be the case for a loan in the form of a mortgage on the property) he usually asks the spouse of the borrower (or any other party who might later claim an interest) to sign the guarantee as well, and for the charge over the property to extend over future loans or extensions as well. Do not be fooled. This is like a blank cheque for the borrower (perhaps your husband) to increase the commitment later without needing to consult you – all backed by your signature to guarantee it! Make sure you understand what you sign and that the limits to your risk you require, now or in the future, cannot be exceeded.

### Should I Run A Business In My Own Name Or Form A Limited Company? How Is It Best To Operate If It Is A Joint Venture With A Friend?

You will need professional advice to make sure your business affairs are properly organised. Work with an accountant and/or solicitor but make sure you also talk to some people in business to find out the real snags. Subsequent changes can be ruinously expensive. Generally, professional people look more towards partnerships, whereas commercial or industrial undertakings find advantages in the limited company format.

You must have a weather eye as a business develops that your potential personal liability is always one you can still meet. Take steps before it goes beyond, that will keep your risks within what you can afford. Consider whether your enterprise could be vulnerable to litigation for product or service liability, which may be potentially crippling. Internationally, as well as in the U.K., the law is in the process of tightening up on this area of business, so you must keep yourself appraised of the current position. The specialists have plenty of solutions; never leave yourself exposed.

Chapter 19 gives additional information about limited companies.

# PART TWO

# 12

# BANKRUPTCY

## Who Can Go Bankrupt?

Only an individual can go bankrupt. The legal term that is used when a limited company goes "bust" is liquidation. This can be voluntary or compulsory and Chapter 19 gives more detail. If you are running a business in your own name, or are the owner, or share ownership or responsibility for, any firm which is not a limited company (e.g., partnerships, associates, etc.) you are liable to be made personally bankrupt if that enterprise cannot pay its debts. That co-proprietor(s) may have hugely differing personal assets which when sold up will produce disproportionate contributions towards the total debts will not be of concern to creditors. The normal thing they can and do do, is to go for the richest where they reckon the assets are.

## Partnerships

Entire families (parents and grown-up children included) have been known to be dragged into personal bankruptcy when businesses fail that they have operated as partners. Without a shadow of a doubt partnership bankruptcies can be the most distressing and upsetting of all. You need very convincing reasons to adopt the partnership format in

business, not to mention remarkable judgment of the quality
of fellow partners.

The law governing partnerships is extremely complex but
this is not the place to go into intricate detail. Suffice to say
that people can sometimes find themselves *deemed* to be
partners in a business even though they did not realise it and
did not have any written or spoken partnership agreement.
Whenever people are working together to make a shareable
profit there is a possibility they might be considered
partners. A good example is when one spouse is running a
shop but the other regularly assists even though not formally
associated with the business. A Court may take the view that
they are essentially in partnership and make them both
bankrupt.

### Bankruptcy Impending

Bankruptcy of an individual usually builds up very slowly. If
business failure is involved too, it can be rapid, for example
when a building contractor loses very heavily on a big
contract that he is undertaking. A major danger in all
bankruptcies however, lies in how slow those under threat so
often are to realise that bankruptcy is looming. Serious debt
problems tend to lead to paralysis of judgment as the debtor
desperately tries to think up ways to avoid the inevitable
conclusion.

A bankruptcy petition is a demand that you pay ALL your
debts in full, *not just the one(s) listed on the petition*.

Many debtors seem to have no idea that this is how the law
works. The crippling totality of this fact escapes their
attention until it is all too late.

It is no use assuming that if you can pay enough into the
Court to satisfy the petitioning creditor you might stave off
bankruptcy; it doesn't work that way. Nor is it the slightest
use to assume that because you know you would be able to
show assets sufficient to cover the whole lot of your debts,
the Court will not make you bankrupt. They almost
certainly will. Their duty is to the creditors, to make sure
they *do* get their money at once. They have no reason to

listen to promises that you will sell things and pay up soon. They bankrupt you to make sure.

Turning up at the Court with enough money to pay *everybody*, then and there, including Court costs, would not necessarily save you either. Under present law there does not seem to be enough leeway to allow a Court any choice about making you bankrupt. They are obliged to do so regardless, though changes presently being considered in the law may make it more flexible in this regard in the future.

## The Need To Avoid Bankruptcy

Please look at the case histories in Chapter 21 should you wish further evidence of the necessity to try and keep out of bankruptcy. Even if it means selling your family home it might be worth it to save your dignity and self-respect. Bankruptcy as you can see all through this book is an executioner's axe which, as well as clearing your every asset, effectively kills off many legal and civil rights.

If you are petitioned for bankruptcy there may be some eleventh hour action worth trying. A visit to the creditors at once must be top of the list. See Chapter 7. Next you should contact your local official receiver's office and ask if any alternative arrangement can be made. It may or may not be too late to have an administration order (Chapter 10) arranged if you are dealing with a County Court; or a scheme on the lines described in Chapter 11 under "Informal Arrangement etc." might be possible if you can get the agreement of all your creditors. You would have to pay the costs of having your estate administered by a third party, but the official receiver should be able to indicate to you if he feels such arrangements are appropriate. Official receivers are listed as such in the telephone book or your local County Court or Citizens Advice Bureau will help you find the address of your nearest office.

You could also seek professional advice from an accountant willing to risk that you can afford it. Some specialise in bankruptcy work and a preliminary discussion should cost nothing. Firms of accountants who are not

specialists in this are unlikely to be much use to you. Make
sure the individual you are taking advice from has first-hand
knowledge. Seek such an expert through your Citizens
Advice Bureau. If you have difficulty in obtaining first-rate
help contact the Association of Bankrupts – address in
Chapter 1, page 26 – which maintains a list of solictors and
accountants around the country prepared to advise debtors.
Do not be afraid, ashamed, or so foolish as not to ask for
help. When you are in a difficult financial impasse you need
support. An adviser on bankruptcy matters is not found on
every street corner, so you will have to make a real effort to
find the right people and get the best advice.

# 13

# PREPARING FOR
# BANKRUPTCY

Many bankruptcies can be compared with an approaching express train which always seems to be a long way off until it hurtles round the final bend at great speed. Debtors are shocked and surprised to find suddenly that their affairs are taken and placed in the hands of an official receiver. Others are aware early on and take various actions to try to protect themselves from its worst effects.

Some such steps are illegal but there is every sense in protecting yourself with allowable measures. Reading this book should give you an appreciation of the sorts of things which might apply in your case. Of the things people try to do when they think they are going bankrupt the most common is to try and get rid of possessions by giving them or selling them cheaply to friends or relatives, with the intention of getting them back later. Such action is unlawful; not surprisingly the law is very strict about it, besides allowing the official receiver to recover any such assets.

Bankruptcy law places fairly stringent limits on the possessions a bankrupt is allowed to keep. Nevertheless official receivers and trustees in bankruptcy (see page 135), are allowed some discretion in practice. This is because individual needs vary so much. A man with children and an elderly relative in his household is unlikely to be deprived of household possessions unless they are luxury items of great value. A single man in a smart suburban home may have his prize possessions carted away. Thus in the nature of things there is an arbitrary element as to how you may be treated.

There is no escaping the emotional pain of having to admit

a complete stranger to your home to inspect and list your personal possessions, many of which may shortly be taken off you. There is no getting away from the fact that in Great Britain, bankruptcy still brings with it a social stigma. But please take heart to strengthen your spirits through the worst. There is life after bankruptcy, although it seems hard to see this at the time. Many bankrupts recover to go on and find fame and fortune. You may well be one of them.

**Joint Bank Accounts**
As a bank will freeze all bank accounts you have at the point of bankruptcy, your partner to a joint account may have insuperable problems if it is his or her only bank account. You should make sure that person makes separate arrangements.

**Wills**
Be warned that families have faced ruin when a non-bankrupt parent has failed to make a Will or to have an existing one rewritten for the perhaps indefinite period that their other half will remain an undischarged bankrupt. The non-bankrupt parent dies and the trustee in bankruptcy scoops the pool, leaving children all but destitute. Have a solicitor draw up an appropriate new Will ready to sign the moment bankruptcy strikes.

Any money willed to a bankrupt from whatever source can be taken by the trustee, so appropriate legal action needs to be taken to avoid sad and unforeseen consequences.

# 14

# PROCEDURE IN BANKRUPTCY

There are only two ways in which you may be made bankrupt. Filing your own petition is one; the other is via a petition from a creditor.

## Filing Your Own Petition

You may file your own petition in bankruptcy, normally in the local County Court. You will have to pay a fee; your local official receiver's office will explain how to proceed.

Such a course however, is unlikely to be rational or logical. People do it because of the emotional and psychological pressures they feel, exacerbated because of harassment by creditors. If you feel under this sort of pressure to make yourself bankrupt, or perhaps honour-bound in some way, it will be worth visiting your official receiver's office before making any hasty decision. You might be able to find out a great deal just on the telephone. Ask to speak to an assistant official receiver or a chief examiner. (Junior examiners may not have the necessary experience to help you.) There should be someone knowledgeable there who can at least indicate what other options might be available, though you can hardly expect direct advice. There is also a bankruptcy administration section of the insolvency service of the Department of Trade and Industry in London who can provide a wealth of information for you, simply on the telephone. Directory enquiries can find the Department of Trade and Industry number for you if necessary.

A good look at the alternatives is likely to reassure you considerably and may well persuade you not to go hurrying along to present your own petition in bankruptcy. Try not to allow a stream of Court orders from creditors to panic you into precipitating your own bankruptcy. It will almost always be the worst option you could take.

**Creditor's Petition**

One or more creditors can ask a Court to make you bankrupt. They may act jointly. You must owe a minimum amount of money laid down by law but you are hardly likely to be petitioned for less. At present the minimum total is £750.00. It is not necessary for a creditor to serve a bankruptcy petition on you in person. If it is served at your last known address it will be deemed properly served. You can therefore be made bankrupt in your absence. People have been known to return from holiday to find themselves bankrupted.

Once a creditor petitions for your bankruptcy there will be a Court hearing to decide whether or not to make you bankrupt.

You must attend otherwise the Court can make an order for your arrest. Be warned that failure to co-operate with any part of the proceedings in bankruptcy means you can be punished in many ways, including being held in bankruptcy for life.

If you are made bankrupt and you think you ought not to have been you can apply to have the bankruptcy notice rescinded. You must appeal immediately because strict time limits apply.

**The Receiving Order**

When a creditor petitions for bankruptcy a receiving order is first made which freezes a debtor's assets until formal adjudication of bankruptcy takes place shortly after. The receiving order stage is expected to disappear when new legislation comes into force. If a receiving order is made against you and you can act quickly to find the funds to pay all your debts, or agree some alternative arrangement with your creditors, then you may still avoid bankruptcy. However, under most circumstances bankruptcy is inevitable once a receiving order is made. If you petition your own bankruptcy then you are adjudicated bankrupt immediately and there is no receiving order.

**Adjudication Of Bankruptcy**
Once you have been made bankrupt the Court orders many of your affairs to be taken out of your hands. Most of your property legally comes under control of the official receiver. Within 24 hours unless it is a weekend, someone from his office will call on you to make a preliminary list of all your property and assets. You will be warned not to move or try to sell anything. All your business papers and books will be taken. If you want to retain copies have them photocopied; otherwise you may have difficulties later on in trying to get access to them. A notice of your bankruptcy will be posted in the London Gazette, a national publication sent to most public libraries and financial institutions to make sure that anyone who thinks you owe them money can hear about it and make a claim against your estate.

You have to give the official receiver a list of all your creditors. They will all be informed and will therefore become aware that, eventually, a proportionate share of your remaining assets will be all they can hope to get. They are no longer allowed to harass you and you should direct any who do contact you to the official receiver. Complain to him if anyone will not leave you alone. Any judgment orders made against you earlier no longer have effect but you must still pay Court fines and/or maintenance orders. Thus a bankruptcy notice closes down your financial affairs. In addition you are no longer allowed to sue anyone you believe owes you money. All such matters are placed under the control of a third party.

## Examination And Statement Of Affairs

Once you have been made bankrupt the next stage is that you must submit for examination. Normally you will be required to attend at the official receiver's office. The duty of the examiner is to satisfy himself that he has obtained full details of all your property and liabilities, and that he has a full account from you as to the cause of the bankruptcy. You can be questioned in great detail about all aspects of your life including any divorces that you have been involved in and any other matters that are relevant. Understandably, many bankrupts find these examinations humiliating and distressing. Sometimes they have to return again and again to the official receiver's office for further questioning. If you have insufficient money to go a long distance ask the official receiver if he can make you a travelling allowance. Cooperate fully with the examination however unpleasant you find the experience. Messing around is only going to delay your eventual discharge from bankruptcy and that is the last thing you are going to want by the end.

## The Creditors' Meeting

Shortly, all your creditors will be invited to attend a meeting at the official receiver's office. You have to be present although you may not be called in. Some bankrupts assume they will have the right to address their creditors at this meeting. This is not so but your creditors can put questions to you, which you are obliged to answer, for example if they suspect you are hiding anything. In most cases however, no creditors bother to attend; they simply send a postal vote suggesting who they would like to have appointed as your trustee. Attending the creditors' meeting can therefore amount to little more than sitting in a corridor for half an hour while the official receiver deals with the papers and votes that creditors have submitted.

The main purpose of a creditors' meeting is to appoint a trustee to dispose of your estate. He or she will be empowered to sell your assets and share out the proceeds by means of proportionate dividends to each creditor. A trustee is usually an accountant in private practice who specialises in such matters. Once appointed the trustee takes over from the official receiver. You will be answerable to the trustee with regard to all your property and income and you are obliged to co-operate. The creditors might also appoint a Committee of Inspection, consisting of a few creditors who will supervise the trustee and decide how much he or she is to be paid. The trustee normally works on a percentage basis of all the money collected and distributed. If you have too few assets to make the involvement of such a trustee worthwhile the official receiver will act as your trustee. He or she is paid out of a general fund so it does not matter if the official receiver cannot recover all costs.

## Arrangements For Your Discharge And Regarding Your Income Meanwhile

Discharge from bankruptcy is yet far off though the registrar may give some directions or indication for a timetable of events. He may suggest a date after which the matter can be reconsidered. In Chapter 17 we have a look at discharge in more detail. Meanwhile he might direct you to make a regular contribution to your bankrupt estate, which may soak up every scrap of spare income you may have. This can range from nothing, if you are presently unemployed, to a substantial slice of any appreciable earnings, and it can be enforced by Court order if necessary, perhaps using an attachment of earnings order (see page 95).

All these formalities being completed you are free, apart from the restrictions imposed by your trustee and the law, to resume and get on with your life. The next Chapter will discuss difficulties you may have as an undischarged bankrupt.

## Public Examinations

At one time every bankrupt had to undergo a public examination in Court. These days they only take place for bankruptcies where there are extremely large liabilities, or where dishonesty is suspected. Nonetheless you may get a letter calling you to Court on a particular day for public examination and you must attend. Very often the style of such a letter is only a formality and vestige of the past. Another letter arrives just before the date stating that the public examination has been dispensed with, or, when you arrive at the Court, the official receiver asks to forego it and this is granted on the nod.

If you are publicly examined you will be put on oath to answer truthfully and honestly all questions put to you by the official receiver or your creditors. It can be quite an ordeal. The official receiver tends to adopt a line of questioning that draws out all your mistakes with no mention of efforts you may have made to repay your debts. Newspaper reporters are sometimes present. They invariably headline the most sensational parts and this can lead to a somewhat distorted report in the press about which there is not a lot you can do.

You are in no position to respond evasively to the questioning. If the registrar decides that you are being less than truthful or co-operative he can adjourn the hearing. Unless you toe the line at a resumed hearing these draconian powers mean that you could be kept in bankruptcy for the rest of your life.

Assuming you have not been shown to have flouted the law – in which case a stay in some grey-bar hotel may later be decreed, or perhaps a fine – public examination is followed by the registrar's decisions about discharge etc, in the same way as ordinary cases noted earlier.

# 15

# PROBLEMS OF BEING AN UNDISCHARGED BANKRUPT

You lose a number of legal rights as a bankrupt. From a legal point of view you become a sort of "non-person". The control of your estate is vested in the official receiver or later in a trustee, with the legal right to dispose of your property and assets. You cannot interfere. It will be up to that person to decide whether to sue anyone for money you believe you are owed. (Action you had already started would have been automatically suspended upon your being declared bankrupt.) He will not do so unless there is an extremely high chance of success. If he does decide against taking a particular legal action one of your creditors may negotiate with him to obtain the "right of action" instead. This might be useful if, say, one of your creditors is a friend or relative willing to help you but you can no longer sue people yourself. However, your champion will be assuming a risk of failure and costs already declined by a specialist.

If you hold certain public offices you have to resign. This would apply to Members of Parliament, local councillors, or anyone holding a position of authority that concerns public policy. You can no longer hold a responsible post involving handling finances. Thus solicitors and accountants for example, would be stripped of their professional status and right to practise. Even after a discharge you can meet enormous difficulties being re-admitted to professional bodies.

**The Marital Home**
Perhaps the most painful thing to face for a married

bankrupt is loss of the family home with the consequent upset and trauma. If you are single and own your home it will be sold straightaway and almost without question. The same may happen if you are married. The difference is in how an array of possible complications can turn the process into an even bigger nightmare, particularly for separated or divorced couples.

A spouse is normally entitled to half share in the family home no matter which of your names ownership may be in. Unless you are both bankrupted the Court will decide on this basis, just how much each of you is entitled to from the sale.

Whichever of you is *not* bankrupt may need to take swift legal action to establish and defend their share of any surplus remaining after outstanding mortgage repayments – a first legal charge – have been paid. Unfortunately, if you are *both* being made bankrupt (e.g. where you had been working in a business partnership which foundered), you lose all the house.

Unequal contributions to the purchase of a home can give rise to unique sets of problems only possible to sort out with specialist legal advice. Take the case of George and Ann Wilson:

When George and Ann married they bought a house costing £30,000. Ann put her £10,000 life savings down as the deposit and they took out a joint mortgage in both names for the balance of £20,000. Shortly after they married George set up in business in his own name marketing computer software but cut-throat competition eventually drove him out of business – bankrupt. Most of the time that George was trying to succeed in building up his firm Ann was working and contributing her half-share to the mortgage repayments, however they now have two tiny children and George has had the entire mortgage round his neck for some months.

You can imagine there are endless variations of this very complex kind of problem. In Ann's position you need to inform the trustee at once what share of the house you are claiming and to be ready to defend your claim at law if necessary. Legal aid may be granted to help you on this. Do not just sit back and expect things to sort themselves out. A trustee has to lay claim to the maximum share of the property that he can, and, to the extent his application is not defended, the Court may be inclined to support him.

Ironically, when a house is mortgaged to very nearly its full value, you may be more likely to be able to retain your family home. An apparently simpler case than George and Ann's is that of Tom and Mary, who have just started buying their own house on an equal joint mortgage. Nevertheless the position needs close attention immediately if future problems are to be avoided.

In terms of a forced sale their house is reckoned to be worth £35,000 but £34,000 is still owed when Tom goes bankrupt. There are no other special complications and it seems clear that Tom and Mary should have equal half shares in the equity of the home. Technically, the trustee is entitled to sell the house and claim Tom's share of equity surplus over and above the mortgage, yet the cost for him would possibly exceed the proceeds.

As Tom cannot pay his half of the mortgage the building society is entitled to call it in and repossess the house anyway; however, if Mary can support the whole mortgage and keep the repayments intact, it is most unlikely to do so with undue haste.

Mary should negotiate with the trustee as early as possible to buy out Tom's share of the house, including the small hypothetical surplus he could otherwise go for by having the house sold. This is assuming she can also afford to maintain the entire mortgage on a permanent basis. At the same time she needs the agreement of the building society for the mortgage to be rewritten solely under her own name, and for this to be properly formalised. She will have to pay all the legal and other costs of this transfer just as in any normal house purchase. The problem if Mary doesn't do this if she could and wants to do so, is that the trustee will register a charge against the property at the Land Registry. Then if the value of the house rises the trustee can force its sale later on. Or if Tom and Mary decide to sell to take the profit, the trustee can demand Tom's share of the extra that comes out. All this would become doubly complicated in trying to evaluate whatever additional mortgage repayments Mary had made by the time the trustee pulled the plug out.

If the position on your home is complex like in these examples you need to find a solicitor well-versed in this backwater of law. Unfortunately there are few around and you may need to search hard.

Still further sorts of difficulty afflict the common law spouse. The law is in such a fluid state concerning their rights and how they become established, that frankly, only a specialist solicitor can advise about their position.

At the time of writing, Parliament is discussing the possibility of allowing a bankrupt and his family to be able to apply to the Court to remain in the family home for a number of years after bankruptcy before its sale would be forced. This may or may not become law. You will need to check on the present position with the official receiver.

### Gas And Electricity

When you are made bankrupt any gas or electricity supplies in your own name can be cut off immediately. You can have your supplies restored by arranging to have pre-payment "slot" meters installed, or by finding a guarantor for future payments. Alternatively it may be appropriate to have these services transferred into your spouse's name. Make arrangements before being cut off, if possible.

### Telephone

If your telephone account is very large when you are made bankrupt it will be cut off as soon as the telephone company is informed by the official receiver. With a small account they might not cut you off so instantly. If you depend on the telephone you can usually make some sort of arrangement to keep it. Ask the telephone company what help they suggest to make this possible.

### Bank Accounts And Savings

All your money in banks, building societies or other savings media will be frozen, held-over to be distributed by the official receiver or trustee. Saleable securities will be sold likewise.

Although you may find it difficult you are free to open another bank account after you are made bankrupt. Since you must tell the bank you are bankrupt if you obtain credit there beyond a specified figure (see page 128), and the bank is therefore obliged to inform the official receiver (because he may be entitled to any money you deposit), there is little point in secrecy about your bankruptcy. If your spouse has a separate bank account it will probably be watched to see that you are not channelling money through it in defiance of the rules. It is far more sensible to keep the bank and the receiver fully informed so that a new bank account for legitimate current use which they can inspect at will is not going to cause you any further problems.

## Fines And Maintenance Orders

Whilst most of a bankrupt's debts become the responsibility of the official receiver, there are two important exceptions. You have to pay any fines imposed by a Court. You must also continue to pay maintenance that has been backed by a Court order.

## Inheritances

It can be very distressing to discover that generous relatives were unaware that these pass straight to your trustee or official receiver, or that they didn't have the opportunity to alter their Wills. If your parents, for example, are planning to leave you well-looked-after for the ultimate benefit of their grandchildren, they will need to see a solicitor to make sure their Wills allow for the fact of your bankruptcy, so that the legacy will be safe from the receiver. Specialist, professional advice is vital for them on this. Note that if they were to die without a Will (intestate) family money, which they might have been assuming would automatically pass to you, could slide into the receiver's hands by default. Thus a proper Will can be essential.

## Your Pension Fund

One of the very few assets of a bankrupt that cannot be touched! It should remain intact to provide for you in retirement. However, if your pension is already being paid to you before you are discharged, that *income* may be subject to your trustee claiming that some of it be paid over to your bankrupt estate.

## Life Assurance Policies

Life assurance policies with a savings element will be seized and cashed in for their surrender value by the receiver or trustee. If a policy has no cash value and is only payable on death you can keep it in force if you wish. Thus a bankrupt can still have his life assured for his spouse's benefit.

You need to be careful how the policy is organised. The *owner* of the policy must be someone other than the bankrupt, in this case your spouse. The proceeds of the policy must be payable directly to that person in the event of your death, so that the trustee in your bankruptcy cannot get his hands on them.

Where both husband and wife are bankrupt it is much more difficult to provide life assurance protection. It may be possible to overcome the problems but that is a matter calling for top-grade specialist advice to see that the results would meet your needs without snags you are not prepared to risk, and that any arrangements you made conformed with bankruptcy law.

## Credit

There is a limit to the amount of future credit a bankrupt can obtain without telling a potential creditor that he/she is bankrupt, as was pointed out earlier. Your official receiver will tell you the present limit. If you break the rules you can be fined or jailed. However, as long as you tell a creditor that you are a bankrupt, there is no limit to the amount of credit you can be given. This is because the creditor then knows you may be an exceptional risk. Fortunately it is quite common for creditors to trust people who they know are bankrupt especially when they enjoy friendly relations and mutual respect. To be safe you would be wise to ask your prospective creditor to put in writing that he knows you are a bankrupt, or you could write to him explaining you are a bankrupt and keep a copy. This should protect you from the creditor, or his successors, ever denying he knew you were a bankrupt.

## Earnings

You will be expected to make payments to the trustee during the period before you are discharged if your earnings are higher than necessary for you to meet basic needs. He has the power to apply to the Court and obtain an order for you to make these payments if you challenge his demands. Sometimes the Court will make an attachment of earnings order, which means *your employer* has to hand over part of your wages to the trustee. However, in practice, such Court directions are unusual and if you make a reasonable offer that you can afford, your trustee is unlikely to bother you any further. People whose only income is from Social Security benefits are hardly ever expected to pay anything in this way.

If you find you cannot keep up with the payments write to your trustee explaining why and offer to pay a smaller amount. He is likely to accept rather than having to apply to the Court for its decision – unless your request is obvious nonsense.

## Obtaining Mortgages

It is virtually impossible for a bankrupt to obtain a mortgage. Even if you did your trustee could sell the property if it increased enough in value to make this worth his while. However, there is no need to advertise the fact that you yourself are a bankrupt if your spouse is in a position to obtain a mortgage in his or her own name. Otherwise, you and your family will have to make do with rented or loaned accommodation until you receive your discharge.

### Offences That Can Be Committed
The main offence that a bankrupt can commit is to obtain credit without disclosing that he/she is an undischarged bankrupt. Other offences are to conceal any property you own, or, to conceal debts due to, as well as from you. It is an offence to fail to keep proper books and accounts of a business, or to conceal these from the official receiver.

You can be imprisoned for serious offences. More often fines are imposed, especially on minor breaches of the law.

### Carrying On In Business
A bankrupt cannot normally be a director of a limited company, or a public company, or be financially liable in the formation of some new enterprise.

Because of this official receivers usually try to discourage bankrupts from continuing in business and many of them will give bankrupts the impression that it is illegal to do so. This is not always the case. A bankrupt can sometimes run a business under his own name. However, depending what it is, the Court's official blessing may be required. This you would have to find out. A Court can be on difficult ground withholding a reasonable request for such permission as may be required by law, so it is a matter worth investigation if you are interested.

The main problems you would face in running your business would be practical ones. Because of your bankruptcy you may have difficulty obtaining credit. (Remember, you must tell your creditors that you are bankrupt.) You will also be at a disadvantage because most of your assets and property have been taken. If your business is successful your trustee is entitled to milk the profits, so if you do more than eke out a living, you are going to have some pretty tough negotiating to do to survive his demands. Nevertheless, with the application of common sense, plenty of bankrupts have managed to rebuild their lives trading as bankrupts under their own names.

**The Position Of The Spouse Of A Bankrupt**
If a forced sale of your home results from bankruptcy of
your better half you are entitled to claim any possessions
that belong to you. This might well be more than a half
share; it depends which of you may have contributed most as
you built them up. Your share of the value of the house itself
is usually the biggest item by far and it may be worth doing
some research to see what size of claim you might have,
based on settlements which have been upheld in similar
circumstances in the past. Check; don't just take the
receiver's word for it.

As the unwittingly injured party it's often worth adopting
a strongly assertive approach with the official receiver
and/or the trustee. Trustees especially, tend to take the
easiest line of action. If they know you are determined and
persistent in demanding your rights you will probably be
treated lots better than someone who gives in to them too
easily. In the nature of things the major household
breadwinner has the greatest chance of success in claiming
relevant ownership but don't let that quell your stamina;
hold out for the best deal you can get. This is one of the many
grey areas in bankruptcy about which the law is not very
clear. A lot of decisions are made by rule of thumb so make
sure they are made to your advantage.

**The Psychological Trauma Of Bankruptcy**
Bankruptcy can bring with it great emotional and psychological problems because of the sense of personal failure that
stalks the loss of all your possessions and sometimes a
business as well. As pressures build up marriages come
under strain and often break up, multiplying the problems
by a quantum leap.

People react differently to bankruptcy depending on their
natures and personalities but many bankrupts talk about
feeling like lepers and wanting to crawl into a corner to hide.

The existence of a "bankruptcy neurosis" – i.e. the
breakdown of proper judgment as bankruptcy approaches –
is widely acknowledged. Less well known is the existence of
what – supported by so much I have seen at close hand – I
will call a "bankruptcy illness".

Having met and helped bankrupts over many years I believe that the shock of bankruptcy for many people, brings with it its own sort of breakdown. Not only is the bankrupt afflicted by this shock but the immediate family and wider family often suffers as well.

For certain types of individual the tortured internal feelings, perhaps attended by unrealistic sensitivity to the public humiliation (however misplaced) lead to a seemingly impossible burden of despair. For some this will be the greatest debt burden of all. Friends and family need to be aware that this can become a burden which may not find relief till months or even years after day-to-day problems have been resolved. Suicide is likely to be contemplated. In extreme cases the person does take his or her own life, adding tragedy to disaster.

A bankrupt and his family need a great deal of psychological help and practical support. Sadly, in our society, this is often lacking. The family home is a "bonding unit" and its loss can place almost intolerable pressure on you all. There are no easy solutions to these family ramifications of bankruptcy but I recommend you seek all the support you can find and accept help from any quarter.

If one member of a family is pitched deep in gloom through bankruptcy, or merely fails to show much ability to bounce back to their former self, do not be afraid to ask if they ever feel suicidal about it all. A close friend of the family may be better placed to do this for you. You can get advice on how to broach the subject from the Samaritans in your area. (See local phone book.) Or, you may be able to suggest to the person concerned to make their own contact with the Samaritans about his or her despair, either by phone or (daytime) visit. They will not help anyone financially but for anyone suffering emotional pain it is a 365 days a year, 24 hour, entirely voluntary organisation. No appointments are needed. Without complete confidentiality it could not exist, so you need not worry on that score. You do not have to reach a suicidal condition to qualify. Samaritans befriend the despairing whatever the level. They are people like you and me, who happen to give some of their time in order to listen to and to support others. The experience which has been built up in doing this has meant that tens of thousands of people from all walks of life have been able to be supported through distress and crisis back to restored happiness.

If you are close to anyone who has made a suicide attempt, take notice; it must almost certainly have been a deep cry for help. Keep an eye and enlist all the assistance you can find, including medical advice. On the subject of medical aid during depression or despair please also look at Chapter 9, page 89.


## Getting Rehoused

Warn your local council housing department what is happening at the earliest opportunity. See page 32.


## Claiming Benefits

Most bankrupts are self-employed people whose businesses have failed. They are independently minded and used to standing on their own two feet and they often find it humiliating to ask for state benefits. It is not an easy task to present yourself at a DHSS office to tell some public official that you are bankrupt and need help.

If it is holding you back, please swallow your pride; your dependants, *including you*, do not deserve further destruction on account of such feelings, honourable or justifiable as they may be. You will in time come through this difficult period and rebuild. And when you do, remember you will probably be paying back into the system far more than you presently need, not to mention what you may have paid into it in the past. So consult Chapter 8 of this book now and set about claiming all the benefits to which you are entitled.


## Getting A Job

Many bankrupts, understandably, give up further ambitions of running their own businesses and seek a job working for someone else at least for the time being. Unfortunately the stigma of bankruptcy is such that some employers will not take on a bankrupt. Others will be more understanding and not hold bankruptcy against you. You need to play your cards close to your chest and use common sense about whether or when, and how, to tell a potential employer about your bankruptcy. Usually it's difficult to avoid anyway but my advice is do, early on, without making too big a thing of it. This way you should avoid disappointment with prejudice blocking your path just when all your hopes are raised.

I could quote many examples which prove how well bankrupts can overcome the obstacles and carve out good careers for themselves as employees but shortage of space prevents that pleasure. Suffice to add that bankrupts are often very skilled and imaginative, with a great deal to offer a future employer.

### A General Hint

Wear your bankruptcy as a badge. This will be much easier than if you try to hide your feelings about the experience, hard as it may be to believe that to begin with. You thereby get everything out in the open and help yourself to be positive about dealing with your immediate problems. Look the world squarely in the eyes and 99% of your worries will lift, enabling you to get on with your life.

# 16

# HOW A BANKRUPT ESTATE IS DEALT WITH

**The Official Receiver**
As we have seen in earlier chapters this is the officer who will take control of your financial affairs immediately you are made bankrupt in Court. He or she is a powerful figure who is both an officer of the Court and an employee of the Department of Trade and Industry. If your property and assets are of little value the official receiver may act as your trustee as well. (See page 120.)

**The Trustee**
If there are considerable assets a separate trustee will be appointed to take over control on behalf of the official receiver. The trustee is nearly always an accountant who specialises in insolvency matters. He also, is an officer of the Court and so has considerable power.

**Charges In Bankruptcy**
Before your creditors receive a dividend all the legal costs of dealing with your bankruptcy have to be paid. Additionally the Department of Trade levies various costs against your estate. The fees of your trustee are another prior charge and when you add everything up, the total expenses just for the "mechanics" of the bankruptcy machine are horrendous. Plenty of bankrupts who thought their assets were more than enough to pay everyone out have been stunned to discover that after all these charges, creditors wound up with

nothing at all. Admittedly this happens partly because assets are allowed to be sold practically for "scrap" value. What is doubly disheartening is to see the wide-boys rife in the wings, rapidly coining rich pickings out of your goods knocked out to them at absurd prices, but that's the way life is going to be until the government grapples with this problem properly.

## How To Deal With The Trustee

The office of your trustee may be many miles from your home and you might only deal with him by letter or through one of his agents.

Unhappily I have often seen adverse relationships develop between bankrupts and their trustees. It is not unnatural to have strong feelings against someone who is about to sell you up, possibly lock, stock *and* barrel but to bite your tongue and establish an atmosphere of friendliness and co-operation is the only sensible route. A trustee has some limited discretion as to how to deal with your affairs. Therefore be firm but polite by all means, but get the person on your side if at all possible.

Do put forward any ideas you have about how your affairs could be handled; to do this in writing may achieve greater impact. Try not to view the trustee as some distant shadowy figure; try to make a friend. Trustees have been known to give references to bankrupts. A few even help find them jobs.

## Release Of Your Trustee

The trustee is legally responsible for your affairs until he applies to the Court to be released. This may take place before your discharge or afterwards.

You might still have some property that has not been sold by the trustee at the time of your discharge, e.g. your house. He can still be in a position to sell any of these assets later, and you may need advice as to what you yourself can or can't do with them meanwhile.

# 17

# OBTAINING A DISCHARGE

## What Is A Discharge?

When you are discharged from your bankruptcy you are no longer responsible for repaying any debts that remain unless there are matters still to be cleared up by the trustee. You have a fresh start. You are free to obtain credit, run a business or whatever, although under new legislation pending at the time of writing, you may be barred from company directorships for several years, so you must check the present position.

Sometimes conditional discharges are given. Here the discharge is granted in return for the formal making over of some of your future income to the trustee for subsequent distribution.

## How Long Is It Before A Discharge Is Granted?

The new law mentioned above may also affect the discharge system so you will need to double-check. Until such changes reach the statute book there are three ways to obtain a discharge:

(1) Automatic discharge: This is granted at the time of adjudication and means you will be discharged automatically from your bankruptcy after 5 years (expected to change to 3 years with the new legislation).

(2) Automatic review: This normally means the Court will simply review your bankruptcy after 5 years have elapsed. Taking account of your then income and whatever you might have been paying regularly to the trustee the Court

will then decide whether or not to postpone your discharge any longer. How long it will be before you reach this stage can depend a lot on your own co-operation; so do give it.

(3) Applying early: You are free at any time, on payment of a fee, to apply for an early discharge. If you are turned down, you can try again later. You will need to show that your bankruptcy is causing you exceptional hardship, such as preventing you obtaining a job. Early discharges usually have conditions attached such as continuing to make a regular payment to your bankruptcy estate.

   If you have the good fortune to get into a position to repay all your debts as well as the bankruptcy administration and Court costs then you can apply to have your bankruptcy annulled. This releases you from bankruptcy immediately and means for all intents and purposes you have never been bankrupt.

## Proposed Changes

The new laws mentioned above may lead to automatic discharge for all first-time bankrupts after 3 years, rather than so much being at the Court's discretion as before.

   Some of the more inhuman aspects of bankruptcy law, will however remain. For example if you do not assist sensibly with the proceedings (in the Court's view) or you have gone bankrupt for a second time you will still be at risk of being held in bankruptcy for life. Antagonise the Court to the point where it stops trying to resolve your problems and you've had it, and will probably die bankrupt.

# 18

# HOW TO COMPLAIN AND HOW TO TAKE LEGAL ACTION

If you are being treated badly by officialdom complain in the first place directly to the person or Court who has taken the action that you feel aggrieved about. Sometimes bankrupts use the wrong channels through failing to appreciate just how to get at the responsible individual(s). For example the only way a decision of a Court can be reversed or changed is by the Court. It is no use complaining to your official receiver or trustee about such a decision. Go to the Court office and ask them how you apply to have the decision changed. (See also page 97.) In bankruptcy matters there are very strict time limits about appeals so act quickly or the law may deny you the opportunity.

Do not be put off if the clerks at the Court do not understand bankruptcy procedure. Many of them lack much bankruptcy experience and they may try to put you off rather than admit this to you. Some of them are much better at lording spurious superiority over members of the public than they are at knowing their jobs. Therefore be prepared to be very firm about the fact that you wish to appeal and that you are entitled to proper answers.

Enlist the help of a friend if you need to polish up a written complaint and make sure it remains objective as well as explicit. Hyperbolic writing will not help you. If you are the sort who gets overheated face-to-face ask someone who is good at keeping calm whilst standing firm, to come along with you to do most of the talking.

If your trustee was ignoring your complaining to him or her you would go back to the official receiver. Official receivers are officers of the Court as well as being answerable as employees to the Department of Trade and Industry. So the thing to do if you experience undue trouble despite your protest to the individual concerned, is to write to the Chief Justice of the Court and/or to the Inspector General of Bankruptcy of the Insolvency Service, c/o the Department of Trade and Industry in London. You can get his address by calling directory enquiries, or you can ask at the official receiver's office. Should none of this draw the appropriate response, then contact your Member of Parliament. Most MPs are very good at assisting bankrupts and sorting out administrative and bureaucratic tangles. In Chapter 2, I discussed how to contact them, page 30.

### Legal Action
Legal aid is currently rarely available in bankruptcy actions, although there are some signs that this is changing. It is most likely to be granted if it was already allowed in some earlier related Court proceedings, in which case the aid may be extended. To set about obtaining legal aid please refer to Chapter 2, page 33 and Chapter 8, page 80. In the absence of legal aid the question of whether to employ a solicitor to complain will depend on the nature of the difficulty as well as whether you will be able to make sure he is paid. Chapter 10 looks at the pros and cons of engaging solicitors.

# 19

# LIMITED LIABILITY COMPANIES

A private limited liability company (Ltd after the name) is a separate legal entity from the people who own and/or manage it. If you are a director or shareholder (or both, as is common in private limited companies) then your personal responsibility for the debts of such a company is basically limited to whatever you may have paid (or agreed to pay) for any part of the share capital in issue which you own in your name. The company is responsible for its own debts. A public limited company (plc) is similar in that the most money members of the public who buy shares can lose in the event of compulsory liquidation, is whatever sum they invested. However plc companies are outside our scope here.

A company may own and buy property and assets. If it fails then only the property and assets registered or purchased in the company's name can be sold to pay creditors. Although shareholders' original investments are lost unless there is anything left over right at the end, and they are likely to lose any loans they might have made to the company, no other personal property or assets of any of its directors can be touched.

This is the favoured form of operation for many businessmen. Every businessman should give very careful thought to seeking this sort of protection and discuss the matter with a knowledgeable accountant.

In legal terms a Ltd (or plc) company does not go bankrupt. It becomes insolvent and eventually goes into (voluntary or compulsory) liquidation. The equivalent of a successful bankruptcy petition is known as a winding up order. Being placed in the hands of the receiver is a last step before liquidation. Occasionally a firm climbs out of receivership back to solvency but it is rare and need not concern us here.

## Warning

So far as company directors are concerned their safety may not be as watertight as implied by the explanations so far. Like so many things legal, snags can puncture your assumptions mercilessly. For example, the signing of a personal guarantee by a director negates the limitation of personal responsibility *for that director*. He or she may well have to stump up whatever is stipulated in the guarantee *regardless of the other directors' positions*. If it is an unlimited guarantee, that could be up to his 'last penny'. For more information about personal guarantees, see page 107.

It is not unknown for a director of a Ltd company to lose his marital home through a bank managing to persuade a Court to grant them a charge over the dwelling despite the Ltd status of the insolvent company. Unscrambling the details of just how this has been done might or might not reveal inadequate legal advice in a particular case but the bank moves on by threatening a possession order for eviction (which it would almost certainly get if it needed to).

One intention of legislation wending its way through Parliament as I write, is to *remove the freedom from personal liability of a director* if it is found he or she allowed trading to continue despite knowing the company was already, or was bound to become, insolvent. How this may be enacted and policed is not yet clear so the reader must keep in touch with events up-to-date.

Be warned then that Ltd status may not be all that it seems, even though it remains the most sensible format under which to trade for most types of business.

## Director Compensation

A company director may be entitled to a redundancy

payment if the company concerned becomes insolvent, unless unusual circumstances apply. Technically he is an employee and should enjoy the same status as other employees referred to at the end of Chapter 8.

# 20

# SCOTLAND – DIFFERENCES IN PROCEDURE

The English and Scottish legal systems mirror each other in most ways so the general advice in this book applies very much the same in either country. However there are some major differences in procedures that are followed. Whereas in England bankruptcy always involves action by a Court, Scotland has a system of "informal bankruptcy" which has been used at least as often as formal sequestration – the Scottish legal term for bankruptcy. There are two ways in Scotland by which an informal bankruptcy can presently be arranged without involving the Courts:

**Informal Bankruptcy In Scotland**
(1) You can make an agreement with your creditors so that they will accept only a part of what you owe them. In return they agree that you will then be free from the rest of your debts. This method known as a "composition contract" is cheap to administer. However it tends not to be used much because no official independent third party exists to administer it. This makes it extremely difficult to organise, as well as to get such agreements from your creditors. It compares somewhat with an Informal Arrangement in England so have a look at Chapter 11 on the subject.

(2) You can hand over all your property and assets to a third party acceptable to everyone involved, usually a solicitor or an accountant, to hold on behalf of your creditors. You sign a trust deed which is usually in a standard form and which removes basic title to the assets from you.

You should look carefully at the form to understand its precise effect. It will both provide for the trustee to be appointed and require that you co-operate with him. As long as your creditors give these arrangements their legal blessing, you will then be free from the rest of the debts that the sale of your assets does not cover. However, any creditor who does not extend his agreement to the scheme may still apply to have you sequestrated.

### Sequestration

Sequestration works in a very similar way to English bankruptcy except that there is no official receiver. The equivalent work of the official receiver is carried out under the supervision of a Court.

As well as differences in bankruptcy procedure, there are technical differences in dealing with debt problems generally compared with the English system. So while the principles outlined in this book can usually be applied in Scotland the Scottish reader will have to relate the advice to his own legal system.

Scottish readers also need to be aware that new insolvency legislation is being planned for their country, due for introduction shortly. To find out how the latest position may affect you is therefore likely to be essential and should be checked with a solicitor.

# 21

# THE BANKRUPTCY MACHINE AT WORK

I have reserved this last Chapter for some case histories, adapted to preserve anonymity for those involved.

## Michael's Story

Michael was born in a German speaking part of Czechoslovakia. When Germany invaded in 1939 he was arrested at the age of 18 for "anti-German activities" and he spent the rest of the war incarcerated in a Nazi concentration camp. Miraculously he survived and returned home to rebuild the family business which produced plastic products of all sorts. When the Communists took over in Czechoslovakia he fell out of favour with the authorities and was forced to flee to Great Britain.

In England he married and set up a successful manufacturing business which went from strength to strength until it was struck by recession. Michael had stood as personal guarantor for the debts of the firm from an early stage, something he was to regret when it finally crashed. Prior to the crash Michael says he was the victim of countless sleepless nights. At that time he was being constantly hounded by bailiffs.

As a result of his various guarantees he was made personally bankrupt. His debts were so large that he was made the subject of a public examination. This lasted over 12 months because of several adjournments. He was also examined in private. Altogether, he was asked over 2,500 questions.

For over 30 years Michael had been a wealthy, highly respected and well-known industrialist employing hundreds of people. His trustee demanded and obtained by means of a Court order all his possessions. He lost his home, the money he had received in compensation for damage to his health in the concentration camp, and all his life assurance policies were cashed up and taken off him. At the age of over 60 he found himself penniless and without a roof over his head. Twelve months before his bankruptcy he had given his physically handicapped daughter several thousand pounds as a down payment for a car fitted with special hand controls. The trustee demanded repayment of this too, and but for the intervention of a relative who paid the money, a sale of the car would have been enforced.

With the help of his family he has been able partly to rebuild his life and he now lives in a rented house with his wife and daughter. He has managed in a small way to re-establish his former business and has reached the point where he is again earning a living.

Michael says he found the bankruptcy procedures humiliating and inhuman – bordering on the intolerable. He says that a society such as ours should be ashamed of creating and tolerating such injustice. While his bankruptcy experience did not in any way match the physical pain and degradation he experienced in the concentration camp he says that nonetheless the emotional and mental pain he experienced was almost unendurable. Without the support of his family he feels he could not have come through the experience.

### Jane's Story

Jane was an accountant who in the past had dealt with many liquidations and bankruptcies; she was employed by a practice that specialised in such matters. She had often heard the cry of the debtor, "But I don't owe as much as that", to which her stock answer was always an unsympathetic: "I'm afraid your affairs are in such a mess you don't realise just how much you do owe".

Twenty-five years ago her husband then in the coal-mining industry was found to be suffering from pneumoconiosis. They decided he would be better away from the mines. He was then in his early forties and because no great opportunities were open elsewhere to someone of his age they resolved to set up their own business. They decided to sell their home to provide the capital for the business.

Jane and her husband bought a small grocery shop and Jane gave up accountancy to assist her husband. The business flourished and soon her husband was the owner of three large self-service stores. They also enjoyed the ownership of a beautiful private residence. However, although they both worked for long hours and spent little on themselves as the business expanded, they never again made the ratio of net profit that they had made when working together in the corner shop without having to employ staff.

They discovered that in self-service retailing, shoplifting was rife and that a large percentage of the staff seemed to regard their chosen perks as a right. Several times Jane caught employees clearing large orders through the checkouts whilst only ringing a few pence up on the tills. They tried to prosecute both shoplifters and staff but found this to be a waste of time because it only brought bad publicity on the shops. So instead the few thieves they caught were either sacked or banned from the shops.

After being established for nearly ten years they suddenly began to have difficulties with their cash flow and found they had a rapidly increasing overdraft at the bank. In desperation they sold one of the shops for a knockdown price but found this only afforded temporary relief. Jane was shortly to realize that the situation could not be saved. Their home had been on the market without a bite for six months and attempts to sell the two remaining shops had failed.

After spending a miserable Christmas, they decided to file their own bankruptcy petitions. Jane was advised by her solicitor not to file her own petition as well (although Jane had the right to sign cheques, all the shops and their home were in her husband's name), but she felt she ought to, to support him, and that it would help. In any case, she reasoned that because she had assisted her husband in the business she would eventually be deemed to be a partner and not to file her own petition would only draw the matter out. She believed it would be better to settle everything immediately.

This was the beginning of 10 long years of great difficulties. Jane's engagement ring was removed from her finger and the trustee later sold it for 5 per cent of the value that Jane had placed upon it. Their home was sold but fetched only what was owing on the mortgage, despite the fact that a firm offer (which subsequently lapsed because the buyer could not wait) had at last been made for their asking price on the day they filed their petitions. The beautiful furnishings, most of which had been bought before their business venture, were virtually given away at auction.

At the time of filing the bankruptcy petitions, Jane knew that their assets more than covered their liabilities. She had kept the books and knew that on balance they only owed £14,000. She was horrified to learn that claims made by their creditors totalled getting on for double that amount. The Department of Trade officials did not appear to take any notice of Jane's ledgers or her protests and they accepted most of the claims as made. Jane and her husband lost everything and were left with less than £1 between them.

Jane returned to her work in the accountancy profession and her husband found work in a factory. They managed to rent a hovel of a home that no-one else was desperate enough to take. They furnished it from second-hand shops. Two years later their house nearly fell down about them and in the emergency they were allocated a council flat in a high-rise block.

The public hearing took place soon after the bankruptcy petitions were filed and no order was made regarding future earnings. After the hearing Jane's husband wanted to move to another area but Jane would have none of it. She insisted that they had done nothing "wrong" and they they should not run away but rebuild their lives in the same city.

Because of the nature of her work, although a bankrupt, Jane was given permission to own a car and operate a bank account. From this account Jane made voluntary payments into their bankruptcy estate.

After being allocated the council flat every penny they could spare was spent on furnishing and decorating. Jane even obtained credit from a furnishing company, having told them she was a bankrupt which she had to do. By five years later they had their home the way they liked it and Jane began saving for a new car. Eventually she bought that car for cash and they even had a few hundred pounds in a building society.

At this time Jane believed they had managed to rebuild their lives successfully.

Then out of the blue they received a letter from the Department of Trade asking them to attend for interview at the local official receiver's office. There, they were told that bankrupts are not allowed to own anything. Jane pointed out that she had been given permission to own a car and to operate a bank account. The official receiver told her that the car should only be a runabout and that she had not been given permission to hold a building society account. He also knew to the last penny what they had in the bank. He said he would need to inspect their home and revalue the furnishings.

The outcome of his investigations was that the money in the building society account was taken, although a small amount in Jane's bank current account was left intact. The car was valued and they were given the opportunity to buy it back from the receiver. The same applied to their furnishings; these had to be paid for by monthly instalments but at least they were given the guarantee that once they had bought them back they would not be foreclosed on again. However, they were warned not to buy anything more or to accumulate any savings prior to their discharge, because any of it would also be liable to be taken.

After this experience Jane made sure that until their discharges eventually came they kept rigidly to all these rules. They had to face the cost of buying back her car and furnishings which came to an appalling £4,500.

They moved twice after their discharge and have finally

been able to rebuild their lives. First they bought a run-down terraced cottage and worked long and hard to modernize it. They sold it at a considerable profit – more than they had hoped for – and this enabled them to buy a pleasant secluded house in another area.

Jane wishes now that she had listened to her husband when he said he wanted to move to another area immediately after the bankruptcy because her honourable desire really only brought about ten long years that neither of them could ever wish to relive.

They keep their skeleton in a well-locked cupboard and no-one around them now knows of their past apart from their bank. Throughout the entire period of bankruptcy they had always used this same bank and had been given a great deal of support. The bank knew all about their background but, kept properly in the picture as it was at all times, never refused them credit facilities.

During the course of her work after she had returned to accountancy, Jane dealt with a client who was obviously going bankrupt. On the pretext of preparing accounts Jane wrote to all the client's creditors asking them to verify their debts. At the same time she instructed her client to incur no more credit. She thus obtained written proof of every debt her client had.

A few weeks later Jane's client filed his own bankruptcy petition. The claims against him by his creditors were well above the true total.

At the same official receiver's office that had been dealing with her own case, Jane succeeded in having these claims corrected to the true total on behalf of her client. She noted however, that again *no action* was taken against the creditors who had put in false claims. She also succeeded in helping to ensure that her client's assets were sold for a reasonable amount. In the event he managed to clear his debts and was not ultimately adjudged bankrupt. He had little left in the way of material goods but he had at least retained his good name and self-respect.

The case was not easy and it took up a huge amount of Jane's time but she believes that it was only her first-hand experience that gave her the insight and knowledge to win through with that client.


## Tom's Story

Tom was an ex-Inspector of taxes who decided after 20 years in the Civil Service to buy a modest family hotel business in a holiday resort. Tom was very successful and was soon able to buy an adjoining building to enlarge the business. He rapidly rose to prominence in the local community and became the head of the local association of hoteliers, speaking for them on matters of mutual interest.

Tom was opposed to a new VAT tax that was levied on small hoteliers which he believed was unfair and engaged in a campaign to try and change matters, writing letters to many Members of Parliament and so forth. In protest, Tom neglected filling in his returns although he did pay any assessments that were sent to him by the Customs and Excise.

Eventually the Customs and Excise presented a bankruptcy petition against Tom for arrears of VAT that Tom disputed. His only debts were £700 claimed by the Customs and Excise and £3,500 in other trade debts. Tom owned all his hotel and furnishings including the addition he had made and he estimated the whole as being worth well over £30,000. He had £1,000 in the bank and owned his own small house as well, worth roughly £12,000.

Before Tom realised what was happening he was adjudicated bankrupt by the Court for non-payment of the VAT debt. A trustee was appointed who immediately sent round a furniture van and took away all the hotel furniture, Tom estimated that the furniture was worth £5,000. It was sold at auction for £600. This had the effect of putting Tom out of business immediately.

Tom refused to assist his trustee, maintaining that he had been illegally and unjustly treated. The trustee sold the hotel for £10,000 despite Tom's protests. The money in Tom's bank account was also taken. The total fees charged by the trustee came to nearly £3,500. All Tom's debts were paid and the few thousand pounds' surplus was returned to him.

As a result of the bankruptcy, his wife left him and Tom now lives alone. Tom maintains that all his debts and the trustee's fees could easily have been paid, simply by selling his £12,000 house. He maintains his protest to this day keeping up a vigorous campaign. Tom had always tried to live a respectable life and fought for his country during the war. He is shattered by this experience which has ruined his life and business. He had no previous idea of the brutal process that he feels he has been the victim of and says that he will spend the rest of his days protesting.

Tom believes that all the bankruptcy machinery in Great Britain needs reforming. He has been to Court to try to get the injustice he believes he himself has suffered rectified. All he was told that he should be grateful that all his debts have been paid and the bankruptcy annulled.

The truth is that Tom was never bankrupt in the normal sense. He was *bankrupted* only because of the wretched system, which allows that to be done. He also blames the Customs and Excise for making an example of someone like him who was trying to stand up to them, in their determination to bring small hoteliers into line over filling in VAT returns. He believes they made unwarranted use of a sledgehammer to crack a nut. He will never forgive his government for the way he has been allowed to be treated.

# APPENDIX OF
# USEFUL ADDRESSES

Various organisations are able to help debtors with specific problems even though they may be unable to provide financial aid. The reader is encouraged to contact them where appropriate.

**Age Concern**
Bernard Sunley House,
60 Pitcairn Road,
Mitcham, Surrey.

**Alcoholics Anonymous**
11 Redcliffe Gardens,
London, SW10.

**Child Poverty Action Group**
1 Macklin Street,
London, WC2.

**Gingerbread**
(For single parents.)
35 Wellington Street,
London, WC2.

**National Association of
Citizens Advice Bureaux**
115 Pentonville Road,
London, N1.

**National Marriage
Guidance Council**
76A New Cavendish Street,
London, W1.

**Samaritans**
(In local phone book.)

**Shelter**
157 Waterloo Road,
London, SE1 8XF.

# INDEX

# OTHER GREAT PAPERFRONT BOOKS

*Each uniform with this book*

## DIVORCE – The Things You Thought You'd Never Need To Know

Jill Black, barrister and law lecturer, translates the legal mumbo jumbo and officialese surrounding divorce into plain English. She steers the reader calmly and sympathetically through what can be a 'minefield', explains the usual sequence of events and how things are set in motion. Later some case histories and a broad insight into how the courts make their decisions – especially regarding the custody of children, the home and finances – help the reader to appreciate what to expect in his or her own circumstances. Tax considerations are dealt with fully.

## WRITE YOUR OWN WILL

Everyone who is over 18 needs to make a Will. If you are wealthy, or your affairs are complicated, then you should consult a solicitor about it after reading this book, which will guide you as to the questions you should ask. For the rest of us who do not have a great deal to dispose of, the matter is straightforward. If it is simply a question of leaving a modest amount of property or money to the immediate family or to charity, then barrister Keith Best's book contains all you need to make a proper legal Will yourself. There's also a chapter of sample Wills designed to cover most circumstances.

## PROBATE – THE RIGHT WAY TO PROVE A WILL

Keith Best explains clearly and concisely how to apply for Probate (or Letters of Administration if there is no Will) and how to administer the Estate. He lays down the sequence of things to do, and gives some basic advice on more technical matters. The help of a solicitor is not necessary for the majority of simple Estates, but the reader is clearly told the circumstances in which it may be needed.

## THE RIGHT WAY TO APPLY FOR A JOB

Whether you are just leaving school or college, or whether you are unemployed, or if you simply want to improve your prospects with a change of job, Arthur Wilcox gives you all the advice you need.

## BUYING OR SELLING A HOUSE

Written by Michael Llewelyn, estate agent and a Fellow of the Royal Institution of Chartered Surveyors, this book gives comprehensive coverage of the legal and financial pitfalls which beset the home buyer or seller. Covers mortgages, surveys, solicitors and how to sell without an estate agent.

## YOUR BUSINESS – THE RIGHT WAY TO RUN IT

*Daily Mail:* A. G. Elliot's 'sometimes startling advice is worth reading'.

Whether you are going to start your own business or buy some existing enterprise, Elliot gives away all the secrets!

## BOOK-KEEPING THE RIGHT WAY

John G. Whyte-Venables explains the principles of correct book-keeping simply and in a logical sequence. The essential reference tool for those starting in business on their own account.

# OUR PUBLISHING POLICY

## HOW WE CHOOSE

Our policy is to consider every deserving manuscript and we can give special editorial help where an author is an authority on his subject but an inexperienced writer. We are rigorously selective in the choice of books we publish. We set the highest standards of editorial quality and accuracy. This means that a *Paperfront* is easy to understand and delightful to read. Where illustrations are necessary to convey points of detail, these are drawn up by a subject specialist artist from our panel.

## HOW WE KEEP PRICES LOW

We aim for the big seller. This enables us to order enormous print runs and achieve the lowest price for you. Unfortunately, this means that you will not find in the *Paperfront* list any titles on obscure subjects of minority interest only. These could not be printed in large enough quantities to be sold for the low price at which we offer this series.

We sell almost all our *Paperfronts* at the same unit price. This saves a lot of fiddling about in our clerical departments and helps us to give you world-beating value. Under this system, the longer titles are offered at a price which we believe to be unmatched by any publisher in the world.

## OUR DISTRIBUTION SYSTEM

Because of the competitive price, and the rapid turnover, *Paperfronts* are possibly the most profitable line a bookseller can handle. They are stocked by the best bookshops all over the world. It may be that your bookseller has run out of stock of a particular title. If so, he can order more from us at any time—we have a fine reputation for "same day" despatch, and we supply any order, however small (even a single copy), to any bookseller who has an account with us. We prefer you to buy from your bookseller, as this reminds him of the strong underlying public demand for *Paperfronts*. Members of the public who live in remote places, or who are housebound, or whose local bookseller is unco-operative, can order direct from us by post.

## FREE

If you would like an up-to-date list of all Paperfront titles currently available, send a stamped self-addressed envelope to
ELLIOT RIGHT WAY BOOKS, BRIGHTON RD.,
LOWER KINGSWOOD, SURREY, U.K.